Key Stages 1 and 2

of the National Curriculum

London : The Stationery Office

Department for Education
Sanctuary Buildings
Great Smith Street
London SW1P 3BT

January 1995

Sixth impression 1996

ISBN 0 11 270893 5

Prepared by the Department for Education
Printed in the United Kingdom for The Stationery Office
Dd 302251 C100 12/96 9385 5337

CONTENTS

This document brings together in a single volume the revised National Curriculum for 5 to 11 year olds (Key Stages 1 and 2) in England. It covers all the required subjects, namely English, mathematics, science, design and technology, information technology, history, geography, art, music and physical education, and has been produced to aid teachers' planning of the curriculum for Key Stages 1 and 2. The full National Curriculum for each subject, covering all the relevant key stages, is set out in separate documents.

The information that follows is based on the Foreword to the subject documents.

■ The structure of the National Curriculum

The National Curriculum applies to pupils of compulsory school age in maintained schools, including grant-maintained and grant-maintained special schools. It is organised on the basis of four **key stages**, which are broadly as follows*:

	Pupils' ages	Year groups
Key Stage 1	5-7	1-2
Key Stage 2	7-11	3-6
Key Stage 3	11-14	7-9
Key Stage 4	14-16	10-11

In England, the following **subjects** are included in the National Curriculum at the key stages shown:

Key Stages 1 and 2	English, mathematics, science, technology (design and technology, and information technology), history, geography, art, music, and physical education
Key Stage 3	as at Key Stages 1 and 2, plus a modern foreign language
Key Stage 4	English, mathematics, and science; from August 1995, physical education; and, from August 1996, technology (design and technology, and information technology) and a modern foreign language.

For each subject and for each key stage, **programmes of study** set out what pupils should be taught and **attainment targets** set out the expected standards of pupils' performance.

At the end of Key Stages 1, 2 and 3, for all subjects except art, music and physical education, standards of pupils' performance are set out in eight **level descriptions** of increasing difficulty, with an additional description above level 8 to help teachers in differentiating exceptional performance. For art, music and physical education, **end of key stage descriptions** set out the standard of performance expected of the majority of pupils at the end of each key stage. Descriptions of exceptional performance are also provided in art and music at the end of Key Stage 3 and in physical education at the end of Key Stage 4.

■ Special educational needs

The revised National Curriculum provides teachers with much greater flexibility to respond to the needs of pupils with identified special educational needs. The statement on access in the section on Common Requirements increases the scope for teachers to provide such pupils with appropriately challenging work at each key stage. This should help to reduce the instances where the requirements of the National Curriculum need to be modified or disapplied for a pupil, either temporarily by the head teacher's direction or through a statement of special educational needs.

---

* The key stages are defined precisely in section 3(3-6) of the Education Reform Act 1988, as amended by the Education Act 1993

■ Implementation dates

The revised programmes of study and attainment targets for each subject become legal requirements by means of an Order made by the Secretary of State for Education (jointly with the Secretary of State for Wales for some subjects) and come into effect on 1 August 1995 for all year groups in Key Stages 1 and 2.

From this date the existing National Curriculum for Key Stages 1 and 2 for each subject, and the appropriate parts of the associated Department for Education circulars, are superseded.

Department for Education

January 1995

COMMON REQUIREMENTS

■ Access

The programme of study for each key stage should be taught to the great majority* of pupils in the key stage, in ways appropriate to their abilities.

For the small number of pupils who may need the provision, material may be selected from earlier or later key stages where this is necessary to enable individual pupils to progress and demonstrate achievement. Such material should be presented in contexts suitable to the pupil's age.

Appropriate provision should be made for pupils who need to use:

- means of communication other than speech, including computers, technological aids, signing, symbols or lip-reading;
- non-sighted methods of reading, such as Braille, or non-visual or non-aural ways of acquiring information;
- technological aids in practical and written work;
- aids or adapted equipment to allow access to practical activities within and beyond school.

   Judgements made in relation to the level descriptions should allow for the provision above, where appropriate.

■ Information technology

Pupils should be given opportunities, where appropriate, to develop and apply their information technology (IT) capability in their study of English.

■ The Curriculum Cymreig

In Wales, pupils should be given opportunities, where appropriate, in their study of English to develop and apply their knowledge and understanding of the cultural, economic, environmental, historical and linguistic characteristics of Wales.

■ Referencing

The numbers and letters throughout the programmes of study are for referencing purposes only, and do not necessarily indicate a particular teaching sequence or hierarchy of knowledge, understanding and skills.

■ Examples

Examples printed in italics are non-statutory.

* Key Stage 1 pupils in Welsh-speaking classes are exempt from the Key Stage 1 Programme of Study for English.

GENERAL REQUIREMENTS FOR ENGLISH: KEY STAGES 1–4

1. English should develop pupils' abilities to communicate effectively in speech and writing and to listen with understanding. It should also enable them to be enthusiastic, responsive and knowledgeable readers.

a To develop effective speaking and listening pupils should be taught to:

- use the vocabulary and grammar of standard English;

- formulate, clarify and express their ideas;

- adapt their speech to a widening range of circumstances and demands;

- listen, understand and respond appropriately to others.

b To develop as effective readers, pupils should be taught to:

- read accurately, fluently and with understanding;

- understand and respond to the texts they read;

- read, analyse and evaluate a wide range of texts, including literature from the English literary heritage and from other cultures and traditions.

c To develop as effective writers, pupils should be taught to use:

- compositional skills – developing ideas and communicating meaning to a reader, using a wide-ranging vocabulary and an effective style, organising and structuring sentences grammatically and whole texts coherently;

- presentational skills – accurate punctuation, correct spelling and legible handwriting;

- a widening variety of forms for different purposes.

2. In order to participate confidently in public, cultural and working life, pupils need to be able to speak, write and read standard English fluently and accurately. All pupils are therefore entitled to the full range of opportunities necessary to enable them to develop competence in standard English. The richness of dialects and other languages can make an important contribution to pupils' knowledge and understanding of standard English. Where appropriate, pupils should be encouraged to make use of their understanding and skills in other languages when learning English.

3. In Wales, the linguistic and cultural knowledge of Welsh-speaking pupils should be recognised and used when developing their competence in English. Teaching should ensure that such pupils are given access to the full scope of the programmes of study. Provision at Key Stage 2 for pupils in Wales who have not followed the Key Stage 1 Programme of Study for English is given on page 32.

4. Pupils should be given opportunities to develop their understanding and use of standard English and to recognise that:

- standard English is distinguished from other forms of English by its vocabulary, and by rules and conventions of grammar, spelling and punctuation;

- the grammatical features that distinguish standard English include how pronouns, adverbs and adjectives should be used and how negatives, questions and verb tenses should be formed; such features are present in both the spoken and written forms, except where non-standard forms are used for effect or technical reasons;

- differences between the spoken and written forms relate to the spontaneity of speech and to its function in conversation, whereas writing is more permanent, often carefully crafted, and less dependent on immediate responses;

- spoken standard English is not the same as Received Pronunciation and can be expressed in a variety of accents.

Pupils' abilities should be developed within an integrated programme of speaking and listening, reading and writing. Pupils should be given opportunities that interrelate the requirements of the Range, Key Skills, and Standard English and Language Study sections.

Speaking and Listening

◼ 1. Range

a Pupils should be given opportunities to talk for a range of purposes, including:

- telling stories, both real and imagined; imaginative play and drama; reading and listening to nursery rhymes and poetry, learning some by heart; reading aloud;

- exploring, developing and clarifying ideas; predicting outcomes and discussing possibilities;

- describing events, observations and experiences; making simple, clear explanations of choices; giving reasons for opinions and actions.

b Pupils should be given opportunities to consider how talk is influenced by the purpose and by the intended audience. These opportunities should include work in groups of different sizes, and talking and presenting work to different audiences, including friends, the class, the teacher and other adults in the school.

c Pupils should be taught to listen carefully and to show their understanding of what they see and hear by making relevant comments. In considering what has been heard, pupils should be encouraged to remember specific points that interested them, and to listen to others' reactions.

d Pupils should be encouraged to participate in drama activities, improvisation and performances of varying kinds, using language appropriate to a role or situation. They should be given opportunities to respond to drama they have watched, as well as that in which they have participated.

◼ 2. Key Skills

a To communicate effectively, pupils should be taught the importance of language that is clear, fluent and interesting. Building on their previous experience, pupils should be encouraged to speak with confidence, making themselves clear through organising what they say and choosing words with precision. They should be taught to incorporate relevant detail in explanations, descriptions and narratives, and to distinguish between the essential and the less important, taking into account the needs of their listeners. Pupils should be taught conventions of discussion and conversation, *eg taking turns in speaking*, and how to structure their talk in ways that are coherent and understandable.

b Pupils should be encouraged to listen with growing attention and concentration, to respond appropriately and effectively to what they have heard, and to ask and answer questions that clarify their understanding and indicate thoughtfulness about the matter under discussion. They should use talk to develop their thinking and extend their ideas in the light of discussion. They should be encouraged to relate their contributions in a discussion to what has gone before, taking different views into account.

■ 3. Standard English and Language Study

a Pupils should be introduced with appropriate sensitivity to the importance of standard English. Pupils should be given opportunities to consider their own speech and how they communicate with others, particularly in more formal situations or with unfamiliar adults. Pupils should be encouraged to develop confidence in their ability to adapt what they say to their listeners and to the circumstances, beginning to recognise how language differs, *eg the vocabulary of standard English and that of dialects, how their choice of language varies in different situations*. They should be introduced to some of the features that distinguish standard English, including subject–verb agreement and the use of the verb 'to be' in past and present tenses. Pupils may speak in different accents, but they should be taught to speak with clear diction and appropriate intonation.

b Pupils' vocabulary should be extended through activities that encourage their interest in words, including exploration and discussion of:

- the meanings of words and their use and interpretation in different contexts;

- words with similar and opposite meanings;

- word games;

- words associated with specific occasions, *eg greetings, celebrations*;

- characteristic language in storytelling, *eg 'Once upon a time'*.

▥ 1. Range

a Pupils should be given extensive experience of children's literature. They should read on their own, with others and to the teacher, from a range of genres that includes stories, poetry, plays and picture books. Pupils should read their own writing to the teacher and to others.

b Pupils should be introduced to and should read information, both in print and on screen. They should be encouraged to make use of a range of sources of information, including dictionaries, IT-based reference materials, encyclopaedias and information presented in fictional form.

c The materials read and discussed should be used to stimulate pupils' imagination and enthusiasm. They should include some or all of these features:

- interesting subject matter and settings, which may be related to pupils' own experience or extend beyond their knowledge of the everyday;

- a clear viewpoint, with accessible themes and ideas;

- clarity of expression and use of language that benefits from being read aloud and reread;

- language with recognisable repetitive patterns, rhyme and rhythm;

- straightforward characterisation and plot;

- the use of a variety of organisational and presentational techniques;

- illustrations that are visually stimulating and enhance the words of the text.

d The literature read should cover the following categories:

- poems and stories with familiar settings and those based on imaginary or fantasy worlds;

- books and poems written by significant children's authors;

- retellings of traditional folk and fairy stories;

- stories and poems from a range of cultures;

- stories, poems and chants containing patterned and predictable language;

- stories and poems that are particularly challenging in terms of length or vocabulary.

▥ 2. Key Skills

a Pupils should be taught to read with fluency, accuracy, understanding and enjoyment, building on what they already know. In order to help them develop understanding of the nature and purpose of reading, they should be given an extensive introduction to books, stories and words in print around them. Pupils should be taught the alphabet, and be made aware of the sounds of spoken language in order to develop phonological awareness. They should also be taught to use various approaches to word identification and recognition, and to use their understanding of grammatical structure and the meaning of the text as a whole to make sense of print.

b Within a balanced and coherent programme, pupils should be taught to use the following knowledge, understanding and skills.

Phonic knowledge, focusing on the relationships between print symbols and sound patterns. Opportunities should be given for:

- recognising alliteration, sound patterns and rhyme, and relating these to patterns in letters;
- considering syllables in longer words;
- identifying initial and final sounds in words;
- identifying and using a comprehensive range of letters and sounds, including combinations of letters, blends and digraphs, and paying specific attention to their use in the formation of words;
- recognising inconsistencies in phonic patterns;
- recognising that some letters do not always produce a sound themselves but influence the sound of others.

Graphic knowledge, focusing on what can be learned about word meanings and parts of words from consistent letter patterns, including:

- plurals;
- spelling patterns in verb endings;
- relationships between root words and derivatives, *eg help, helpful*;
- prefixes and suffixes.

Word recognition, focusing on the development of a vocabulary of words recognised and understood automatically and quickly. This should extend from a few words of personal importance to a larger number of words from books and the environment. Pupils should be shown how to use their sight vocabulary to help them read words that have similar features. They should discuss alternative meanings of words and phrases.

Grammatical knowledge, focusing on the way language is ordered and organised into sentences (syntax). Pupils should be shown how to use their knowledge of word order and the structure of written language to confirm or check meaning. Pupils should be taught to recognise the value of surrounding text in identifying unknown words. They should be taught to:

- check the accuracy of their reading, attending to whether it sounds right and/or makes sense grammatically;
- reread and/or read ahead passages when the sense has been lost.

Contextual understanding, focusing on meaning derived from the text as a whole. In order to confirm the sense of what they read, pupils should be taught to use their knowledge of book conventions, story structure, patterns of language and presentational devices, and their background knowledge and understanding of the content of a book. They should be taught to keep the overall sense of a passage in mind as a checking device.

c In understanding and responding to stories and poems, pupils should be given opportunities to:

- talk about characters, events and language in books, beginning to use appropriate terminology;

- say what might happen next in a story;

- retell stories;

- explain the content of a passage or whole text;

- choose books to read individually and with others;

- review their reading with their teacher;

- read complete short texts, including playscripts;

- reread favourite stories and poems, learning some by heart;

- hear stories and poems read aloud frequently and regularly, including some longer, more challenging material;

- prepare, present and act out stories and poems they have read.

d Pupils should be taught to use reference materials for different purposes. They should be taught about the structural devices for organising information, *eg contents, headings, captions.*

■ 3. Standard English and Language Study

Pupils should be given opportunities to consider the characteristics and features of different kinds of texts, *eg beginnings and endings in stories.* They should be taught to use their knowledge about language gained from reading, to develop their understanding of standard English.

Writing

■ 1. Range

a Pupils should be helped to understand the value of writing as a means of remembering, communicating, organising and developing ideas and information, and as a source of enjoyment. Pupils should be taught to write independently on subjects that are of interest and importance to them.

b Pupils should be given opportunities to write in response to a variety of stimuli, including stories, poems, classroom activities and personal experience. Pupils should be taught to identify the purpose for which they write and to write for a range of readers, *eg their teacher, their family, their peers, themselves.*

c Pupils should be taught to organise and present their writing in different ways, helpful to the purpose, task and reader. They should be taught to write in a range of forms, incorporating some of the different characteristics of those forms. The range should include a variety of narratives, *eg stories, diaries*; poems; notes, *eg lists, captions*; records, *eg observations*; and messages, *eg notices, invitations, instructions.*

■ 2. Key Skills

a Pupils should be taught to write with confidence, fluency and accuracy. They should be taught to differentiate between print and pictures, to understand the connections between speech and writing, and to learn about the different purposes and functions of written language. Pupils should be introduced to the alphabetic nature of writing and be taught to discriminate between letters, learning to write their own name. Pupils' early experiments and independent attempts at communicating in writing, using letters and known words, should be encouraged.

b Pupils should have opportunities to plan and review their writing, assembling and developing their ideas on paper and on screen. Teachers should, on occasions, help pupils to compose at greater length by writing for them, demonstrating the ways that ideas may be recorded in print. To encourage confidence and independence, pupils should be given opportunities to collaborate, to read their work aloud and to discuss the quality of what is written. Pupils should be helped to make choices about vocabulary and to organise imaginative and factual writing in different ways, *eg a cumulative pattern in a poem, a list of ingredients for a cake.*

c In **punctuation**, pupils should be taught that punctuation is essential to help a reader understand what is written. Pupils should be given opportunities to read their work aloud in order to understand the connections between the punctuation of a sentence and intonation and emphasis. Pupils should be taught to punctuate their writing, be consistent in their use of capital letters, full stops and question marks, and begin to use commas.

d In **spelling**, pupils should be taught to:

- write each letter of the alphabet;
- use their knowledge of sound–symbol relationships and phonological patterns;
- recognise and use simple spelling patterns;
- write common letter strings within familiar and common words;
- spell commonly occurring simple words;
- spell words with common prefixes and suffixes.

Pupils should be taught to check the accuracy of their spelling, and to use word books and dictionaries, identifying initial letters as the means of locating words. They should be given opportunities to experiment with the spelling of complex words and to discuss misapplied generalisations and other reasons for misspellings. Close attention should be paid to word families.

e In **handwriting**, pupils should be taught to hold a pencil comfortably in order to develop a legible style that follows the conventions of written English, including:

- writing from left to right and from top to bottom of the page;

- starting and finishing letters correctly;

- regularity of size and shape of letters;

- regularity of spacing of letters and words.

They should be taught the conventional ways of forming letters, both lower case and capitals. They should build on their knowledge of letter formation to join letters in words. They should develop an awareness of the importance of clear and neat presentation, in order to communicate their meaning effectively.

3. Standard English and Language Study

a Pupils should be introduced to the vocabulary, grammar and structures of written standard English, including subject–verb agreement, and the use of the verb 'to be' in past and present tenses. They should be taught to apply their existing linguistic knowledge, drawn from oral language and their experience of reading, to develop their understanding of the sentence and how word choice and order are crucial to clarity of meaning. Pupils should be given opportunities to discuss the organisation of more complex texts, and the way sentences link together.

b Pupils' interest in words and their meanings should be developed, and their vocabulary should be extended through consideration and discussion of words with similar meanings, opposites, and words with more than one meaning.

KEY STAGE 2 PROGRAMME OF STUDY

Pupils' abilities should be developed within an integrated programme of speaking and listening, reading and writing. Pupils should be given opportunities that interrelate the requirements of the Range, Key Skills, and Standard English and Language Study sections.

Speaking and Listening

◼ 1. Range

a Pupils should be given opportunities to talk for a range of purposes, including:

- exploring, developing, and explaining ideas;
- planning, predicting, and investigating;
- sharing ideas, insights and opinions;
- reading aloud, telling and enacting stories and poems;
- reporting and describing events and observations;
- presenting to audiences, live or on tape.

b Pupils should be given opportunities to communicate to different audiences and to reflect on how speakers adapt their vocabulary, tone, pace and style.

c Pupils should be given opportunities to listen and respond to a range of people. They should be taught to identify and comment on key features of what they see and hear in a variety of media.

d Pupils should be given opportunities to participate in a wide range of drama activities, including improvisation, role-play, and the writing and performance of scripted drama. In responding to drama, they should be encouraged to evaluate their own and others' contributions.

◼ 2. Key Skills

a Pupils should be encouraged to express themselves confidently and clearly. Pupils should be taught to organise what they want to say, and to use vocabulary and syntax that enables the communication of more complex meanings. In discussions, pupils should be given opportunities to make a range of contributions, depending on the activity and the purpose of the talk. This range should include making exploratory and tentative comments when ideas are being collected together, and making reasoned, evaluative comments as discussion moves to conclusions or action. Pupils should be taught to evaluate their own talk and reflect on how it varies.

b Pupils should be taught to listen carefully, and to recall and re-present important features of an argument, talk, presentation, reading, radio or television programme. They should be taught to identify the gist of an account or the key points made in discussion, to evaluate what they hear, and to make contributions that are relevant to what is being considered. They should be taught to listen to others, questioning them to clarify what they mean, and extending and following up the ideas. They should be encouraged to qualify or justify what they think after listening to other opinions or accounts, and deal politely with opposing points of view.

■ 3. Standard English and Language Study

a Pupils' appreciation and use of standard English should be developed by involvement with others in activities that, through their content and purpose, demand the range of grammatical constructions and vocabulary characteristic of spoken standard English. They should be taught to speak with clear diction and appropriate intonation. Pupils should be taught how formal contexts require particular choices of vocabulary and greater precision in language structures. They should also be given opportunities to develop their understanding of the similarities and differences between the written and spoken forms of standard English, and to investigate how language varies according to context and purpose and between standard and dialect forms.

b Pupils should be taught to use an increasingly varied vocabulary. The range of pupils' vocabulary should be extended and enriched through activities that focus on words and their meanings, including:

- discussion of more imaginative and adventurous choices of words;
- consideration of groups of words, *eg word families, the range of words relevant to a topic*;
- language used in drama, role-play and word games.

Reading

■ 1. Range

a Pupils should be encouraged to develop as enthusiastic, independent and reflective readers. They should be introduced to a wide range of literature, and have opportunities to read extensively for their own interest and pleasure, and for information. Pupils' reading should be developed through the use of progressively more challenging and demanding texts. Opportunities for reading should include both independent and shared reading of play scripts and other texts, by groups and the whole class. Pupils working at Levels 1 and 2 should be given access to literature appropriate to their age and maturity.

b Pupils should read and use a wide range of sources of information, including those not specifically designed for children. The range of non-fiction should include IT-based reference materials, newspapers, encyclopaedias, dictionaries and thesauruses.

c Pupils' reading should include texts:

- with challenging subject matter that broadens perspectives and extends thinking;
- with more complex narrative structures and sustained ideas;
- that include figurative language, both in poetry and prose;
- with a variety of structural and organisational features.

d The literature read should cover the following categories:

- a range of modern fiction by significant children's authors;
- some long-established children's fiction;
- a range of good quality modern poetry;
- some classic poetry;
- texts drawn from a variety of cultures and traditions;
- myths, legends and traditional stories.

■ 2. Key Skills

a To increase their ability to read with fluency, accuracy, understanding and enjoyment, pupils should be taught to extend their phonic and graphic knowledge to include more complex patterns and irregularities.

b Pupils should be taught to consider in detail the quality and depth of what they read. They should be encouraged to respond imaginatively to the plot, characters, ideas, vocabulary and organisation of language in literature. They should be taught to use inference and deduction. Pupils should be taught to evaluate the texts they read, and to refer to relevant passages or episodes to support their opinions.

c Pupils should be taught how to find information in books and computer-based sources by using organisational devices to help them decide which parts of the material to read closely. They should be given opportunities to read for different purposes, adopting appropriate strategies for the task, including skimming to gain an overall impression, scanning to locate information and detailed reading to obtain specific information. Pupils should be taught to:

- pose pertinent questions about a topic they are investigating;
- identify the precise information that they wish to know;
- distinguish between fact and opinion;
- consider an argument critically;
- make succinct notes;
- use dictionaries, glossaries and thesauruses to explain unfamiliar vocabulary;
- note the meaning and use of newly encountered words;
- re-present information in different forms.

d Pupils should be taught to use library classification systems, catalogues and indexes.

■ 3. Standard English and Language Study

Pupils should be introduced to the organisational, structural and presentational features of different types of text, and to some of the appropriate terms to enable them to discuss the texts they read, *eg author, setting, plot, format*. They should be encouraged to use their knowledge gained from reading to develop their understanding of the structure, vocabulary and grammar of standard English.

Writing

■ 1. Range

a Pupils should be given opportunities to write for varied purposes, understanding that writing is essential to thinking and learning, and enjoyable in itself. They should be taught to use writing as a means of developing, organising and communicating ideas.

b Pupils should be given opportunities to write for an extended range of readers, *eg the teacher, the class, other children, adults in the school or community, imagined audiences*. They should write in response to a wide range of stimuli, including stories, plays and poems, their interests and experiences, and the activities of the classroom.

c They should be taught to use the characteristics of different kinds of writing, *eg argument, commentary, narrative, dialogue*. The forms in which they write should include imaginative writing, *eg stories, poems, dialogues, drama scripts, diaries*; and non-fiction, *eg reports, instructions, explanations, notes, letters*. They should be taught to use features of layout and presentation.

■ 2. Key Skills

a Pupils should be taught to write in response to more demanding tasks. As pupils write for a wider range of purposes, they should be taught to distinguish degrees of formality in writing for unfamiliar audiences, *eg as appropriate to guidebooks, pamphlets, reviews*. They should be encouraged to make judgements about when a particular tone, style, format or choice of vocabulary is appropriate.

b Pupils should be given opportunities to plan, draft and improve their work on paper and on screen, and to discuss and evaluate their own and others' writing. To develop their writing, pupils should be taught to:

- **plan** – note and develop initial ideas;
- **draft** – develop ideas from the plan into structured written text;
- **revise** – alter and improve the draft;
- **proofread** – check the draft for spelling and punctuation errors, omissions or repetitions;
- **present** – prepare a neat, correct and clear final copy.

Pupils should be encouraged to develop their ability to organise and structure their writing in a variety of ways, using their experience of fiction, poetry and other texts.

c In **punctuation**, pupils should be taught to use punctuation marks correctly in their writing, including full stops, question and exclamation marks, commas, inverted commas, and apostrophes to mark possession.

d In **spelling**, pupils should be accumulating a bank of words that they can spell correctly, and should be taught to check spellings and meanings of words, using dictionaries where appropriate. When looking up words, pupils should be taught to apply their knowledge of initial and subsequent letters and the organisation of dictionaries, including headings, abbreviations and other conventions. They should be taught:

- the meaning, use, and spelling of common prefixes and suffixes;
- the relevance of word families, roots and origins of words;
- alternative ways of writing the same sound;
- the spelling of words with inflectional endings.

Pupils should be taught to:

- spell complex, polysyllabic words that conform to regular patterns, and to break long and complex words into more manageable units, by using their knowledge of meaning and word structure;
- memorise the visual patterns of words, including those that are irregular;
- recognise silent letters;
- use the apostrophe to spell shortened forms of words;
- use appropriate terminology, including vowel and consonant.

e In **handwriting**, pupils should be given opportunities to continue to develop legible handwriting in both joined up and printed styles. As pupils become increasingly confident and independent, they should be encouraged to develop greater control and fluency. They should be taught to use different forms of handwriting for different purposes, *eg print for labelling maps or diagrams; a clear, neat hand for finished, presented work; a faster script for notes.*

■ 3. Standard English and Language Study

a Pupils should be given opportunities to reflect on their use of language, beginning to differentiate between spoken and written forms. They should be given opportunities to consider how written standard English varies in degrees of formality.

b Pupils should be given opportunities to develop their understanding of the grammar of complex sentences, including clauses and phrases. They should be taught how to use paragraphs, linking sentences together coherently. They should be taught to use the standard written forms of nouns, pronouns, verbs, adjectives, adverbs, prepositions, conjunctions and verb tenses.

c Pupils should be taught to distinguish between words of similar meaning, to explain the meanings of words and to experiment with choices of vocabulary. Their interest in words should be extended by the discussion of language use and choices.

ATTAINMENT TARGETS

LEVEL DESCRIPTIONS

The following level descriptions describe the types and range of performance that pupils working at a particular level should characteristically demonstrate. In deciding on a pupil's level of attainment at the end of a key stage, teachers should judge which description best fits the pupil's performance. Each description should be considered in conjunction with the descriptions for adjacent levels.

By the end of Key Stage 1, the performance of the great majority of pupils should be within the range of Levels 1 to 3, by the end of Key Stage 2 it should be within the range 2 to 5 and by the end of Key Stage 3 within the range 3 to 7.

Attainment Target 1: Speaking and Listening

▇ Level 1

Pupils talk about matters of immediate interest. They listen to others and usually respond appropriately. They convey simple meanings to a range of listeners, speaking audibly, and begin to extend their ideas or accounts by providing some detail.

▇ Level 2

Pupils begin to show confidence in talking and listening, particularly where the topics interest them. On occasions, they show awareness of the needs of the listener by including relevant detail. In developing and explaining their ideas they speak clearly and use a growing vocabulary. They usually listen carefully and respond with increasing appropriateness to what others say. They are beginning to be aware that in some situations a more formal vocabulary and tone of voice are used.

▇ Level 3

Pupils talk and listen confidently in different contexts, exploring and communicating ideas. In discussion, they show understanding of the main points. Through relevant comments and questions, they show they have listened carefully. They begin to adapt what they say to the needs of the listener, varying the use of vocabulary and the level of detail. They are beginning to be aware of standard English and when it is used.

▇ Level 4

Pupils talk and listen with confidence in an increasing range of contexts. Their talk is adapted to the purpose: developing ideas thoughtfully, describing events and conveying their opinions clearly. In discussion, they listen carefully, making contributions and asking questions that are responsive to others' ideas and views. They use appropriately some of the features of standard English vocabulary and grammar.

▇ Level 5

Pupils talk and listen confidently in a wide range of contexts, including some that are of a formal nature. Their talk engages the interest of the listener as they begin to vary their expression and vocabulary. In discussion, they pay close attention to what others say, ask questions to develop ideas and make contributions that take account of others' views. They begin to use standard English in formal situations.

▇ Level 6

Pupils adapt their talk to the demands of different contexts with increasing confidence. Their talk engages the interest of the listener through the variety of its vocabulary and expression. Pupils take an active part in discussion, showing understanding of ideas and sensitivity to others. They are usually fluent in their use of standard English in formal situations.

■ Level 1

Pupils recognise familiar words in simple texts. They use their knowledge of letters and sound–symbol relationships in order to read words and to establish meaning when reading aloud. In these activities they sometimes require support. They express their response to poems, stories and non-fiction by identifying aspects they like.

■ Level 2

Pupils' reading of simple texts shows understanding and is generally accurate. They express opinions about major events or ideas in stories, poems and non-fiction. They use more than one strategy, such as phonic, graphic, syntactic and contextual, in reading unfamiliar words and establishing meaning.

■ Level 3

Pupils read a range of texts fluently and accurately. They read independently, using strategies appropriately to establish meaning. In responding to fiction and non-fiction they show understanding of the main points and express preferences. They use their knowledge of the alphabet to locate books and find information.

■ Level 4

In responding to a range of texts, pupils show understanding of significant ideas, themes, events and characters, beginning to use inference and deduction. They refer to the text when explaining their views. They locate and use ideas and information.

■ Level 5

Pupils show understanding of a range of texts, selecting essential points and using inference and deduction where appropriate. In their responses, they identify key features, themes and characters, and select sentences, phrases and relevant information to support their views. They retrieve and collate information from a range of sources.

■ Level 6

In reading and discussing a range of texts, pupils identify different layers of meaning and comment on their significance and effect. They give personal responses to literary texts, referring to aspects of language, structure and themes in justifying their views. They summarise a range of information from different sources.

English

Reading

Level

Descriptions

■ Level 1

Pupils' writing communicates meaning through simple words and phrases. In their reading or their writing, pupils begin to show awareness of how full stops are used. Letters are usually clearly shaped and correctly orientated.

■ Level 2

Pupils' writing communicates meaning in both narrative and non-narrative forms, using appropriate and interesting vocabulary, and showing some awareness of the reader. Ideas are developed in a sequence of sentences, sometimes demarcated by capital letters and full stops. Simple, monosyllabic words are usually spelt correctly, and where there are inaccuracies the alternative is phonetically plausible. In handwriting, letters are accurately formed and consistent in size.

■ Level 3

Pupils' writing is often organised, imaginative and clear. The main features of different forms of writing are used appropriately, beginning to be adapted to different readers. Sequences of sentences extend ideas logically and words are chosen for variety and interest. The basic grammatical structure of sentences is usually correct. Spelling is usually accurate, including that of common, polysyllabic words. Punctuation to mark sentences – full stops, capital letters and question marks – is used accurately. Handwriting is joined and legible.

■ Level 4

Pupils' writing in a range of forms is lively and thoughtful. Ideas are often sustained and developed in interesting ways and organised appropriately for the purpose and the reader. Vocabulary choices are often adventurous and words are used for effect. Pupils are beginning to use grammatically complex sentences, extending meaning. Spelling, including that of polysyllabic words that conform to regular patterns, is generally accurate. Full stops, capital letters and question marks are used correctly, and pupils are beginning to use punctuation within the sentence. Handwriting style is fluent, joined and legible.

■ Level 5

Pupils' writing is varied and interesting, conveying meaning clearly in a range of forms for different readers, using a more formal style where appropriate. Vocabulary choices are imaginative and words are used precisely. Simple and complex sentences are organised into paragraphs. Words with complex regular patterns are usually spelt correctly. A range of punctuation, including commas, apostrophes and inverted commas, is usually used accurately. Handwriting is joined, clear and fluent and, where appropriate, is adapted to a range of tasks.

■ Level 6

English

Writing

Level

Descriptions

Pupils' writing often engages and sustains the reader's interest, showing some adaptation of style and register to different forms, including using an impersonal style where appropriate. Pupils use a range of sentence structures and varied vocabulary to create effects. Spelling is generally accurate, including that of irregular words. Handwriting is neat and legible. A range of punctuation is usually used correctly to clarify meaning, and ideas are organised into paragraphs.

COMMON REQUIREMENTS

■ Access

The programme of study for each key stage should be taught to the great majority of pupils in the key stage, in ways appropriate to their abilities.

For the small number of pupils who may need the provision, material may be selected from earlier or later key stages where this is necessary to enable individual pupils to progress and demonstrate achievement. Such material should be presented in contexts suitable to the pupil's age.

Appropriate provision should be made for pupils who need to use:

- means of communication other than speech, including computers, technological aids, signing, symbols or lip-reading;
- non-sighted methods of reading, such as Braille, or non-visual or non-aural ways of acquiring information;
- technological aids in practical and written work;
- aids or adapted equipment to allow access to practical activities within and beyond school.

  Judgements made in relation to the level descriptions should allow for the provision above, where appropriate.

■ Use of language

Pupils should be taught to express themselves clearly in both speech and writing and to develop their reading skills. They should be taught to use grammatically correct sentences and to spell and punctuate accurately in order to communicate effectively in written English or, when the medium is Welsh, in written Welsh.

■ Information technology

Pupils should be given opportunities, where appropriate, to develop and apply their information technology (IT) capability in their study of mathematics.

■ The Curriculum Cymreig

In Wales, pupils should be given opportunities, where appropriate, in their study of mathematics, to develop and apply their knowledge and understanding of the cultural, economic, environmental, historical and linguistic characteristics of Wales.

■ Referencing

The numbers and letters throughout the programmes of study are for referencing purposes only and do not necessarily indicate a particular teaching sequence or hierarchy of knowledge, understanding and skills.

■ Examples

Examples printed in italics are non-statutory.

KEY STAGE 1 PROGRAMME OF STUDY

The sections of the programme of study interrelate. Developing mathematical language, selecting and using materials, and developing reasoning, should be set in the context of the other areas of mathematics. Sorting, classifying, making comparisons and searching for patterns should apply to work on number, shape and space, and handling data. The use of number should permeate work on measures and handling data.

Using and Applying Mathematics

■ **1. Pupils should be given opportunities to:**

    a use and apply mathematics in practical tasks, in real-life problems and within mathematics itself;

    b explain their thinking to support the development of their reasoning.

Pupils should be taught to:

■ **2. Making and monitoring decisions to solve problems**

    a select and use the appropriate mathematics;

    b select and use mathematical equipment and materials;

    c develop different mathematical approaches and look for ways to overcome difficulties;

    d organise and check their work.

■ **3. Developing mathematical language and communication**

    a understand the language of number, properties of shapes and comparatives, *eg 'bigger than', 'next to', 'before'*;

    b relate numerals and other mathematical symbols, *eg '+', '=',* to a range of situations;

    c discuss their work, responding to and asking mathematical questions;

    d use a variety of forms of mathematical presentation.

■ **4. Developing mathematical reasoning**

    a recognise simple patterns and relationships and make related predictions about them;

    b ask questions including 'What would happen if?' and 'Why?', *eg considering the behaviour of a programmable toy*;

    c understand general statements, *eg 'all even numbers divide by 2'*, and investigate whether particular cases match them.

Number

■ **1. Pupils should be given opportunities to:**

a develop flexible methods of working with number, orally and mentally;

b encounter numbers greater than 1000;

c use a variety of practical resources and contexts;

d use calculators both as a means to explore number and as a tool for calculating with realistic data, *eg numbers with several digits*;

e record in a variety of ways, including ways that relate to their mental work;

f use computer software, including a database.

Pupils should be taught to:

■ **2. Developing an understanding of place value**

a count orally up to 10 and beyond, knowing the number names; count collections of objects, checking the total; count in steps of different sizes, *eg count on from 5 in steps of 2 or 3*; recognise sequences, including odd and even numbers;

b read, write and order numbers, initially to 10, progressing up to 1000, developing an understanding that the position of a digit signifies its value; begin to approximate larger numbers to the nearest 10 or 100;

c recognise and use in context simple fractions, including halves and quarters, decimal notation in recording money, and negative numbers, *eg a temperature scale, a number line, a calculator display*.

■ **3. Understanding relationships between numbers and developing methods of computation**

a use repeating patterns to develop ideas of regularity and sequencing;

b explore and record patterns in addition and subtraction, and then patterns of multiples, *eg 3, 6, 9, 12*, explaining their patterns and using them to make predictions; progress to exploring further patterns involving multiplication and division, including those within a hundred-square of multiplication facts;

c know addition and subtraction facts to 20, and develop a range of mental methods for finding, from known facts, those that they cannot recall; learn multiplication and division facts relating to the 2s, 5s, 10s, and use these to learn other facts, *eg double multiples of 2 to produce multiples of 4*, and to develop mental methods for finding new results;

d develop a variety of methods for adding and subtracting, including using the fact that subtraction is the inverse of addition;

e use a basic calculator, reading the display, *eg use the constant function to explore repeated addition*.

Pupils should be taught to:

■ 4. Solving numerical problems

a understand the operations of addition, subtraction as taking away and comparison, and the relationship between them, recognise situations to which they apply and use them to solve problems with whole numbers, including situations involving money;

b understand the operations of multiplication, and division as sharing and repeated subtraction, and use them to solve problems with whole numbers or money, understanding and dealing appropriately with remainders;

c choose a suitable method of computation, using apparatus where appropriate, or a calculator where the numbers include several digits;

d begin to check answers in different ways, *eg repeating the calculation in a different order or using a different method*, and gain a feel for the appropriate size of an answer.

■ 5. Classifying, representing and interpreting data

a sort and classify a set of objects using criteria related to their properties, *eg size, shape, mass*;

b collect, record and interpret data arising from an area of interest, using an increasing range of charts, diagrams, tables and graphs.

Shape, Space and Measures

■ **1. Pupils should be given opportunities to:**

    a gain a wide range of practical experience using a variety of materials;

    b use IT devices, *eg programmable toys, turtle graphics packages*;

    c use purposeful contexts for measuring.

    Pupils should be taught to:

■ **2. Understanding and using patterns and properties of shape**

    a describe and discuss shapes and patterns that can be seen or visualised;

    b make common 3-D and 2-D shapes and models, working with increasing care and accuracy; begin to classify shapes according to mathematical criteria;

    c recognise and use the geometrical features of shapes, including vertices, sides/edges and surfaces, rectangles (including squares), circles, triangles, cubes, cuboids, progressing to hexagons, pentagons, cylinders and spheres; recognise reflective symmetry in simple cases.

■ **3. Understanding and using properties of position and movement**

    a describe positions, using common words; recognise movements in a straight line, ie translations, and rotations, and combine them in simple ways; copy, continue and make patterns;

    b understand angle as a measure of turn and recognise quarter-turns and half-turns, *eg giving instructions for rotating a programmable toy*; recognise right angles.

■ **4. Understanding and using measures**

    a compare objects and events using appropriate language, by direct comparison, and then using common non-standard and standard units of length, mass and capacity, *eg 'three-and-a-bit metres long', 'as heavy as 10 conkers', 'about three beakers full'*; begin to use a wider range of standard units, including standard units of time, choosing units appropriate to a situation; estimate with these units;

    b choose and use simple measuring instruments, reading and interpreting numbers and scales with some accuracy.

The sections of the programme of study interrelate. Developing mathematical language, reasoning and skills in applying mathematics should be set in the context of the other areas of mathematics. Measurement should be associated with handling data and shape and space. Calculating skills should be developed in number and through work on measures and handling data. Algebraic ideas of pattern and relationships should be developed in all areas of mathematics.

Using and Applying Mathematics

1. Pupils should be given opportunities to:

a use and apply mathematics in practical tasks, in real-life problems and within mathematics itself;

b take increasing responsibility for organising and extending tasks;

c devise and refine their own ways of recording;

d ask questions and follow alternative suggestions to support the development of reasoning.

Pupils should be taught to:

2. Making and monitoring decisions to solve problems

a select and use the appropriate mathematics and materials;

b try different mathematical approaches; identify and obtain information needed to carry out their work;

c develop their own mathematical strategies and look for ways to overcome difficulties;

d check their results and consider whether they are reasonable.

3. Developing mathematical language and forms of communication

a understand and use the language of:

- number;
- the properties and movements of shapes;
- measures;
- simple probability;
- relationships, including 'multiple of', 'factor of' and 'symmetrical to';

b use diagrams, graphs and simple algebraic symbols;

c present information and results clearly, and explain the reasons for their choice of presentation.

4. Developing mathematical reasoning

a understand and investigate general statements, *eg 'wrist size is half neck size', 'there are four prime numbers less than 10'*;

b search for pattern in their results;

c make general statements of their own, based on evidence they have produced;

d explain their reasoning.

■ **1. Pupils should be given opportunities to:**

    a develop flexible and effective methods of computation and recording, and use them with understanding;

    b use calculators, computers and a range of other resources as tools for exploring number structure and to enable work with realistic data;

    c develop the skills needed for accurate and appropriate use of equipment.

    Pupils should be taught to:

■ **2. Developing an understanding of place value and extending the number system**

    a read, write and order whole numbers, understanding that the position of a digit signifies its value; use their understanding of place value to develop methods of computation, to approximate numbers to the nearest 10 or 100, and to multiply and divide by powers of 10 when there are whole-number answers;

    b extend their understanding of the number system to negative numbers in context, and decimals with no more than two decimal places in the context of measurement and money;

    c understand and use, in context, fractions and percentages to estimate, describe and compare proportions of a whole.

■ **3. Understanding relationships between numbers and developing methods of computation**

    a explore number sequences, *eg counting in different sizes of step, doubling and halving, using a multiplication square*, explaining patterns and using simple relationships; progress to interpreting, generalising and using simple mappings, *eg C=15n for the cost of n articles at 15p*, relating to numerical, spatial or practical situations, expressed initially in words and then using letters as symbols;

    b recognise the number relationship between co-ordinates in the first quadrant of related points on a line or in a shape, *eg the vertices of a rectangle, a graph of the multiples of 3*;

    c consolidate knowledge of addition and subtraction facts to 20; know the multiplication facts to 10×10; develop a range of mental methods for finding quickly from known facts those that they cannot recall; use some properties of numbers, including multiples, factors and squares, extending to primes, cubes and square roots;

    d develop a variety of mental methods of computation with whole numbers up to 100, and explain patterns used; extend mental methods to develop a range of non-calculator methods of computation that involve addition and subtraction of whole numbers, progressing to methods for multiplication and division of up to three-digit by two-digit whole numbers;

Pupils should be taught to:

e understand multiplication as repeated addition, and division as sharing and repeated subtraction; use associated language and recognise situations to which the operations apply;

f understand and use the relationships between the four operations, including inverses;

g extend methods of computation to include addition and subtraction with negative numbers, all four operations with decimals, and calculating fractions and percentages of quantities, using a calculator where appropriate;

h understand and use the features of a basic calculator, interpreting the display in the context of the problem, including rounding and remainders.

■ 4. Solving numerical problems

a develop their use of the four operations to solve problems, including those involving money and measures, using a calculator where appropriate;

b choose sequences of methods of computation appropriate to a problem, adapt them and apply them accurately;

c check results by different methods, including repeating the operations in a different order or using inverse operations; gain a sense of the size of a solution, and estimate and approximate solutions to problems.

1. Pupils should be given opportunities to:

a use geometrical properties and relationships in the solution of problems;

b extend their practical experience using a wide range of materials;

c use computers to create and transform shapes;

d consider a wide range of patterns, including some drawn from different cultural traditions;

e apply their measuring skills in a range of purposeful contexts.

Pupils should be taught to:

2. Understanding and using properties of shape

a visualise and describe shapes and movements, developing precision in using related geometrical language;

b make 2-D and 3-D shapes and patterns with increasing accuracy, recognise their geometrical features and properties, and use these to classify shapes and solve problems;

c understand the congruence of simple shapes; recognise reflective symmetries of 2-D and 3-D shapes, and rotational symmetries of 2-D shapes.

3. Understanding and using properties of position and movement

a transform 2-D shapes by translation, reflection and rotation, and visualise movements and simple transformations to create and describe patterns;

b use co-ordinates to specify location, *eg map references, representation of 2-D shapes*;

c use right angles, fractions of a turn and, later, degrees, to measure rotation, and use the associated language.

4. Understanding and using measures

a choose appropriate standard units of length, mass, capacity and time, and make sensible estimates with them in everyday situations; extend their understanding of the relationship between units; convert one metric unit to another; know the rough metric equivalents of Imperial units still in daily use;

b choose and use appropriate measuring instruments; interpret numbers and read scales to an increasing degree of accuracy;

c find perimeters of simple shapes; find practically the circumferences of circles, being introduced to the ratio π; find areas and volumes by counting methods, leading to the use of other practical methods, *eg dissection*.

Handling Data

■ **1. Pupils should be given opportunities to:**

a formulate questions about an issue of their choice, and consider them using statistical methods;

b access and collect data through undertaking purposeful enquiries;

c use computers as a source of interesting data, and as a tool for representing data.

Pupils should be taught to:

Mathematics

Key Stage 2

Handling Data

■ **2. Collecting, representing and interpreting data**

a interpret tables used in everyday life; interpret and create frequency tables, including those for grouped discrete data;

b collect and represent discrete data appropriately using graphs and diagrams, including block graphs, pictograms and line graphs; interpret a wider range of graphs and diagrams that represent data, including pie charts, using a computer where appropriate;

c understand and use measures of average, leading towards the mode, the median and the mean in relevant contexts, and the range as a measure of spread;

d draw conclusions from statistics and graphs, and recognise why some conclusions can be uncertain or misleading.

■ **3. Understanding and using probability**

a develop understanding of probability, through experience as well as experiment and theory, and discuss events and simple experiments, using a vocabulary that includes the words 'evens', 'fair', 'unfair', 'certain', 'likely', 'probably', and 'equally likely';

b understand that the probability of any event lies between impossibility and certainty, leading to the use of the scale from 0 to 1;

c recognise situations where probabilities can be based on equally likely outcomes, and others where estimates must be based on experimental evidence; make or approximate these estimates.

LEVEL DESCRIPTIONS

The following level descriptions describe the types and range of performance that pupils working at a particular level should characteristically demonstrate. In deciding on a pupil's level of attainment at the end of a key stage, teachers should judge which description best fits the pupil's performance. Each description should be considered in conjunction with the descriptions for adjacent levels.

By the end of Key Stage 1, the performance of the great majority of pupils should be within the range of Levels 1 to 3, by the end of Key Stage 2 it should be within the range 2 to 5, and by the end of Key Stage 3 within the range 3 to 7.

■ Level 1

Pupils use mathematics as an integral part of classroom activities. They represent their work with objects or pictures and discuss it. They recognise and use a simple pattern or relationship, usually based on their experience.

■ Level 2

Pupils select the mathematics for some classroom activities. They discuss their work using familiar mathematical language and are beginning to represent it using symbols and simple diagrams. They ask and respond appropriately to questions including 'What would happen if...?'.

■ Level 3

Pupils try different approaches and find ways of overcoming difficulties that arise when they are solving problems. They are beginning to organise their work and check results. Pupils discuss their mathematical work and are beginning to explain their thinking. They use and interpret mathematical symbols and diagrams. Pupils show that they understand a general statement by finding particular examples that match it.

■ Level 4

Pupils are developing their own strategies for solving problems and are using these strategies both in working within mathematics and in applying mathematics to practical contexts. They present information and results in a clear and organised way, explaining the reasons for their presentation. They search for a pattern by trying out ideas of their own.

■ Level 5

In order to carry through tasks and solve mathematical problems, pupils identify and obtain necessary information; they check their results, considering whether these are sensible. Pupils show understanding of situations by describing them mathematically using symbols, words and diagrams. They make general statements of their own, based on evidence they have produced, and give an explanation of their reasoning.

■ Level 6

Pupils carry through substantial tasks and solve quite complex problems by breaking them down into smaller, more manageable tasks. They interpret, discuss and synthesise information presented in a variety of mathematical forms. Pupils' writing explains and informs their use of diagrams. Pupils are beginning to give a mathematical justification for their generalisations; they test them by checking particular cases.

■ Level 1

Pupils count, order, add and subtract numbers when solving problems involving up to 10 objects. They read and write the numbers involved. Pupils recognise and make repeating patterns, counting the number of each object in each repeat.

■ Level 2

Pupils count sets of objects reliably, and use mental recall of addition and subtraction facts to 10. They have begun to understand the place value of each digit in a number and use this to order numbers up to 100. They choose the appropriate operation when solving addition and subtraction problems. They identify and use halves and quarters, such as half of a rectangle or a quarter of eight objects. They recognise sequences of numbers, including odd and even numbers.

■ Level 3

Pupils show understanding of place value in numbers up to 1000 and use this to make approximations. They have begun to use decimal notation and to recognise negative numbers, in contexts such as money, temperature and calculator displays. Pupils use mental recall of addition and subtraction facts to 20 in solving problems involving larger numbers. They use mental recall of the 2, 5 and 10 multiplication tables, and others up to 5×5, in solving whole-number problems involving multiplication or division, including those that give rise to remainders. Pupils use calculator methods where numbers include several digits. They have begun to develop mental strategies, and use them to find methods for adding and subtracting numbers with at least two digits.

■ Level 4

Pupils use their understanding of place value to multiply and divide whole numbers by 10 or 100. In solving number problems, pupils use a range of mental and written methods of computation with the four operations, including mental recall of multiplication facts up to 10×10. They add and subtract decimals to two places. In solving problems with or without a calculator, pupils check the reasonableness of their results by reference to their knowledge of the context or to the size of the numbers. They recognise approximate proportions of a whole and use simple fractions and percentages to describe these. Pupils explore and describe number patterns, and relationships including multiple, factor and square. They have begun to use simple formulae expressed in words. Pupils use and interpret co-ordinates in the first quadrant.

■ Level 5

Pupils use their understanding of place value to multiply and divide whole numbers and decimals by 10, 100 and 1000. They order, add and subtract negative numbers in context. They use all four operations with decimals to two places. They calculate fractional or percentage parts of quantities and measurements, using a calculator where appropriate. Pupils understand and use an appropriate non-calculator method for solving problems that involve multiplying and dividing any three-digit by any two-digit number. They check their solutions by applying inverse operations or estimating using approximations. They construct, express in symbolic form, and use simple formulae involving one or two operations.

■ Level 6

Pupils order and approximate decimals when solving numerical problems and equations such as $x^2 = 20$, using trial-and-improvement methods. Pupils are aware of which number to consider as 100 per cent, or a whole, in problems involving comparisons, and use this to evaluate one number as a fraction or percentage of another. They understand and use the equivalences between fractions, decimals and percentages, and calculate using ratios in appropriate situations. When exploring number patterns, pupils find and describe in words the rule for the next term or nth term of a sequence where the rule is linear. They formulate and solve linear equations with whole number coefficients. They represent mappings expressed algebraically, interpreting general features and using graphical representation in four quadrants where appropriate.

■ Level 1

When working with 3-D and 2-D shapes, pupils use everyday language to describe properties and positions. They measure and order objects using direct comparison, and order events.

■ Level 2

Pupils use mathematical names for common 3-D and 2-D shapes and describe their properties, including numbers of sides and corners. They distinguish between straight and turning movements, understand angle as a measurement of turn, and recognise right angles in turns. They have begun to use everyday non-standard and standard units to measure length and mass.

■ Level 3

Pupils classify 3-D and 2-D shapes in various ways using mathematical properties such as reflective symmetry. They use non-standard units and standard metric units of length, capacity, mass and time, in a range of contexts.

■ Level 4

Pupils make 3-D mathematical models by linking given faces or edges, draw common 2-D shapes in different orientations on grids, and identify congruent shapes and orders of rotational symmetry. They reflect simple shapes in a mirror line. They choose and use appropriate units and instruments, interpreting, with appropriate accuracy, numbers on a range of measuring instruments. They find perimeters of simple shapes, find areas by counting squares, and find volumes by counting cubes.

■ Level 5

When constructing models and when drawing or using shapes, pupils measure and draw angles to the nearest degree, and use language associated with angle. They identify all the symmetries of 2-D shapes. They know the rough metric equivalents of Imperial units still in daily use and convert one metric unit to another. They make sensible estimates of a range of measures in relation to everyday situations.

■ Level 6

Pupils recognise and use common 2-D representations of 3-D objects. They know and use the properties of quadrilaterals in classifying different types of quadrilateral. They solve problems using angle and symmetry properties of polygons and properties of intersecting and parallel lines, and explain these properties. They devise instructions for a computer to generate and transform shapes and paths. They understand and use appropriate formulae for finding circumferences and areas of circles, areas of plane rectilinear figures and volumes of cuboids when solving problems. They enlarge shapes by a positive whole-number scale factor.

Life Processes and Living Things

Work on life processes should be related to pupils' knowledge of animals and plants in the local environment.

Pupils should be taught:

■ **1. Life processes**

a   the differences between things that are living and things that have never been alive;

b   that animals, including humans, move, feed, grow, use their senses and reproduce.

■ **2. Humans as organisms**

a   to name the main external parts, *eg hand, elbow, knee,* of the human body;

b   that humans need food and water to stay alive;

c   that taking exercise and eating the right types and amount of food help humans to keep healthy;

d   about the role of drugs as medicines;

e   that humans can produce babies and these babies grow into children and then into adults;

f   that humans have senses which enable them to be aware of the world around them.

■ **3. Green plants as organisms**

a   that plants need light and water to grow;

b   to recognise and name the leaf, flower, stem and root of flowering plants;

c   that flowering plants grow and produce seeds which, in turn, produce new plants.

■ **4. Variation and classification**

a   to recognise similarities and differences between themselves and other pupils;

b   that living things can be grouped according to observable similarities and differences.

■ **5. Living things in their environment**

a   that there are different kinds of plants and animals in the local environment;

b   that there are differences between local environments and that these affect which animals and plants are found there.

Experimental and Investigative Science

Contexts derived from **Life Processes and Living Things**, **Materials and their Properties** and **Physical Processes** should be used to teach pupils about experimental and investigative methods. On some occasions, the whole process of investigating an idea should be carried out by pupils themselves.

Pupils should be taught:

■ **1. Planning experimental work**

a to turn ideas suggested to them, and their own ideas, into a form that can be investigated;

b that thinking about what is expected to happen can be useful when planning what to do;

c to recognise when a test or comparison is unfair.

■ **2. Obtaining evidence**

a to explore using appropriate senses;

b to make observations and measurements;

c to make a record of observations and measurements.

■ **3. Considering evidence**

a to communicate what happened during their work;

b to use drawings, tables and bar charts to present results;

c to make simple comparisons;

d to use results to draw conclusions;

e to indicate whether the evidence collected supports any prediction made;

f to try to explain what they found out, drawing on their knowledge and understanding.

The requirements in this section of the programme of study apply across **Experimental and Investigative Science**, **Life Processes and Living Things**, **Materials and their Properties** and **Physical Processes**.

Science Key Stage 1

Pupils should be given opportunities to:

■ 1. Systematic enquiry

a ask questions, *eg 'How?', 'Why?', 'What will happen if...?'*;

b use focused exploration and investigation to acquire scientific knowledge, understanding and skills;

c use both first-hand experience and simple secondary sources to obtain information;

d use IT to collect, store, retrieve and present scientific information.

■ 2. Science in everyday life

a relate their understanding of science to domestic and environmental contexts;

b consider ways in which science is relevant to their personal health;

c consider how to treat living things and the environment with care and sensitivity.

■ 3. The nature of scientific ideas

a relate simple scientific ideas to the evidence for them.

Pupils should be taught to:

■ 4. Communication

a use scientific vocabulary to name and describe living things, materials, phenomena and processes;

b present scientific information in a number of ways, through drawings, diagrams, tables and charts, and in speech and writing.

■ 5. Health and safety

a recognise hazards and risks when working with living things and materials;

b follow simple instructions to control the risks to themselves.

COMMON REQUIREMENTS

■ Access

The programme of study for each key stage should be taught to the great majority of pupils in the key stage, in ways appropriate to their abilities.

For the small number of pupils who may need the provision, material may be selected from earlier or later key stages where this is necessary to enable individual pupils to progress and demonstrate achievement. Such material should be presented in contexts suitable to the pupil's age.

Appropriate provision should be made for pupils who need to use:

- means of communication other than speech, including computers, technological aids, signing, symbols or lip-reading;

- non-sighted methods of reading, such as Braille, or non-visual or non-aural ways of acquiring information;

- technological aids in practical and written work;

- aids or adapted equipment to allow access to practical activities within and beyond school.

  Pupils with hearing impairment should be supported, in gaining as much access as possible to the **Sound** sections of the programmes of study, by the use of visual demonstrations of the properties of sounds, for example through the use of oscilloscopes, sound-level meters, speech trainers or musical instruments.

  Pupils with visual impairment should be supported in gaining as much access as possible to the **Light** sections of the programmes of study. Most pupils will be able to take part in practical activities, either by careful use of their residual vision or, for example, by using their knowledge that most light sources produce heat.

  Judgements made in relation to the level descriptions should allow for the provision above, where appropriate.

■ Use of language

Pupils should be taught to express themselves clearly in both speech and writing and to develop their reading skills. They should be taught to use grammatically correct sentences and to spell and punctuate accurately in order to communicate effectively in written English or, when the medium is Welsh, in written Welsh.

■ Information technology

Pupils should be given opportunities, where appropriate, to develop and apply their information technology (IT) capability in their study of science.

■ The Curriculum Cymreig

In Wales, pupils should be given opportunities, where appropriate, in their study of science to develop and apply their knowledge and understanding of the cultural, economic, environmental, historical and linguistic characteristics of Wales.

■ Referencing

The numbers and letters throughout the programmes of study are for referencing purposes only and do not necessarily indicate a particular teaching sequence or hierarchy of knowledge, understanding and skills.

■ Examples

Examples printed in italics are non-statutory.

This attainment target does not apply to pupils in Key Stage 1.

■ Level 1

Pupils sort objects and classify them, demonstrating the criterion they have used.

■ Level 2

Pupils sort objects and classify them using more than one criterion. When they have gathered information, pupils record results in simple tables, block graphs and diagrams, in order to communicate their findings.

■ Level 3

Pupils extract and interpret information presented in simple tables and lists. They construct bar charts and pictograms, where the symbol represents a group of units, to communicate information they have gathered, and they interpret information presented to them in these forms.

■ Level 4

Pupils collect discrete data and record them using a frequency table. They understand and use the mode and median. They group data, where appropriate, in equal class intervals, represent collected data in frequency diagrams and interpret such diagrams. They construct and interpret simple line graphs. They understand and use simple vocabulary associated with probability, including 'fair', 'certain' and 'likely'.

■ Level 5

Pupils understand and use the mean of discrete data. They compare two simple distributions, using the range and one of the measures of average. They interpret graphs and diagrams, including pie charts, and draw conclusions. They understand and use the probability scale from 0 to 1. Pupils find and justify probabilities, and approximations to these, by selecting and using methods based on equally likely outcomes and experimental evidence, as appropriate. They understand that different outcomes may result from repeating an experiment.

■ Level 6

Pupils collect and record continuous data, choosing appropriate equal class intervals over a sensible range to create frequency tables. They construct and interpret frequency diagrams. They construct pie charts. Pupils draw conclusions from scatter diagrams, and have a basic understanding of correlation. When dealing with a combination of two experiments, pupils identify all the outcomes, using diagrammatic, tabular or other forms of communication. In solving problems, they use their knowledge that the total probability of all the mutually exclusive outcomes of an experiment is 1.

Mathematics

Handling Data

Level Descriptions

Materials and their Properties

Work on everyday uses of materials should be related to pupils' knowledge of the properties of the materials and of objects made from them, and to their knowledge of the way changes affect the materials.

Pupils should be taught:

■ 1. Grouping materials

a to use their senses to explore and recognise the similarities and differences between materials;

b to sort materials into groups on the basis of simple properties, including texture, appearance, transparency and whether they are magnetic or non-magnetic;

c to recognise and name common types of material, *eg metal, plastic, wood, paper, rock*, and to know that some of these materials are found naturally;

d that many materials, *eg glass, wood, wool*, have a variety of uses;

e that materials are chosen for specific uses, *eg glass for windows, wool for clothing*, on the basis of their properties.

■ 2. Changing materials

a that objects made from some materials can be changed in shape by processes including squashing, bending, twisting and stretching;

b to describe the way some everyday materials, *eg water, chocolate, bread, clay*, change when they are heated or cooled.

Physical Processes

Work on observable effects should be related to pupils' knowledge of physical phenomena.

Pupils should be taught:

■ **1. Electricity**

a that many everyday appliances use electricity;

b to construct simple circuits involving batteries, wires, bulbs and buzzers;

c that electrical devices will not work if there is a break in the circuit.

■ **2. Forces and motion**

a to describe the movement of familiar things, *eg cars getting faster, slowing down, changing direction*;

b that both pushes and pulls are examples of forces;

c that forces can make things speed up, slow down or change direction;

d that forces can change the shapes of objects.

■ **3. Light and sound**

light and dark

a that light comes from a variety of sources, including the Sun;

b that darkness is the absence of light;

making and detecting sounds

c that there are many kinds of sound and many sources of sound;

d that sounds travel away from sources, getting fainter as they do so;

e that sounds are heard when they enter the ear.

The requirements in this section of the programme of study apply across **Experimental and Investigative Science**, **Life Processes and Living Things**, **Materials and their Properties** and **Physical Processes**.

Pupils should be given opportunities to:

■ **1. Systematic enquiry**

  a ask questions related to their work in science;

  b use focused exploration and investigation to acquire scientific knowledge, understanding and skills;

  c use both first-hand experience and secondary sources to obtain information;

  d use IT to collect, store, retrieve and present scientific information.

■ **2. Science in everyday life**

  a use their knowledge and understanding of science to explain and interpret a range of familiar phenomena;

  b consider the part science has played in the development of many of the things that they use;

  c relate their understanding of science to their personal health;

  d consider ways in which living things and the environment need protection.

■ **3. The nature of scientific ideas**

  a obtain evidence to test scientific ideas in a variety of ways;

  b recognise that science provides explanations for many phenomena.

Pupils should be taught to:

■ **4. Communication**

  a use appropriate scientific vocabulary to describe and explain the behaviour of living things, materials and processes;

  b use standard measures and SI units, *eg metre, newton*, appropriate to their work;

  c use a wide range of methods, including diagrams, drawings, graphs, tables and charts, to record and present information in an appropriate and systematic manner.

■ **5. Health and safety**

  a recognise and assess the hazards and risks to themselves and to others when working with living things and materials;

  b take action to control these risks.

Science

Key Stage 2

Experimental and Investigative Science

Contexts derived from **Life Processes and Living Things**, **Materials and their Properties** and **Physical Processes** should be used to teach pupils about experimental and investigative methods. On some occasions, the whole process of investigating an idea should be carried out by pupils themselves.

Science

Key Stage 2

Experimental
and
Investigative
Science

Pupils should be taught:

1. Planning experimental work

a to turn ideas suggested to them, and their own ideas, into a form that can be investigated;

b that making predictions can be useful when planning what to do;

c to decide what evidence should be collected;

d that changing one factor and observing or measuring the effect, whilst keeping other factors the same, allows a fair test or comparison to be made;

e to consider what apparatus and equipment to use.

2. Obtaining evidence

a to use simple apparatus and equipment correctly;

b to make careful observations and measurements;

c to check observations and measurements by repeating them.

3. Considering evidence

a to use tables, bar charts and line graphs to present results;

b to make comparisons and to identify trends or patterns in results;

c to use results to draw conclusions;

d to indicate whether the evidence collected supports any prediction made;

e to try to explain conclusions in terms of scientific knowledge and understanding.

Work on life processes should be related to pupils' knowledge of animals and plants in the local environment. Work on the variety of life in a habitat should be linked to the reasons for classifying living things.

Pupils should be taught:

■ 1. Life processes

a that there are life processes, including nutrition, movement, growth and reproduction, common to animals, including humans;

b that there are life processes, including growth, nutrition and reproduction, common to plants.

■ 2. Humans as organisms

nutrition

a the functions of teeth and the importance of dental care;

b that food is needed for activity and for growth, and that an adequate and varied diet is needed to keep healthy;

circulation

c a simple model of the structure of the heart and how it acts as a pump;

d how blood circulates in the body through arteries and veins;

e the effect of exercise and rest on pulse rate;

movement

f that humans have skeletons and muscles to support their bodies and to help them to move;

growth and reproduction

g the main stages of the human life cycle;

health

h that tobacco, alcohol and other drugs can have harmful effects.

■ 3. Green plants as organisms

growth and nutrition

a that plant growth is affected by the availability of light and water, and by temperature;

b that plants need light to produce food for growth, and the importance of the leaf in this process;

c that the root anchors the plant, and that water and nutrients are taken in through the root and transported through the stem to other parts of the plant;

reproduction

d about the life cycle of flowering plants, including pollination, seed production, seed dispersal and germination.

Science

Key Stage 2

Life Processes and Living Things

Pupils should be taught:

■ 4. Variation and classification

a how locally occurring animals and plants can be identified and assigned to groups, using keys.

■ 5. Living things in their environment

adaptation

a that different plants and animals are found in different habitats;

b how animals and plants in two different habitats are suited to their environment;

feeding relationships

c that food chains show feeding relationships in an ecosystem;

d that nearly all food chains start with a green plant;

micro-organisms

e that micro-organisms exist, and that many may be beneficial, *eg in the breakdown of waste*, while others may be harmful, *eg in causing disease*.

Materials and their Properties

Work on solids, liquids and gases should be related to pupils' observations of changes that take place when materials are heated and cooled, and to ways in which mixtures can be separated.

Pupils should be taught:

■ 1. Grouping and classifying materials

a to compare everyday materials, *eg wood, rock, iron, aluminium, paper, polythene*, on the basis of their properties, including hardness, strength, flexibility and magnetic behaviour, and to relate these properties to everyday uses of the materials;

b that some materials are better thermal insulators than others;

c that some materials are better electrical conductors than others;

d to describe and group rocks and soils on the basis of characteristics, including appearance, texture and permeability;

e to recognise differences between solids, liquids and gases, in terms of ease of flow and maintenance of shape and volume.

■ 2. Changing materials

a that mixing materials, *eg adding salt to water*, can cause them to change;

b that heating or cooling materials, *eg water, clay, dough*, can cause them to change, and that temperature is a measure of how hot or cold they are;

c that some changes can be reversed and some cannot;

d that dissolving, melting, boiling, condensing, freezing and evaporating are changes that can be reversed;

e about the water cycle and the part played by evaporation and condensation;

f that the changes that occur when most materials, *eg wood, wax, natural gas*, are burned are not reversible.

■ 3. Separating mixtures of materials

a that solid particles of different sizes, *eg those in soils*, can be separated by sieving;

b that some solids, *eg salt, sugar*, dissolve in water to give solutions but some, *eg sand, chalk*, do not;

c that insoluble solids can be separated from liquids by filtering;

d that solids that have dissolved can be recovered by evaporating the liquid from the solution;

e that there is a limit to the mass of solid that can dissolve in a given amount of water, and that this limit is different for different solids.

Physical Processes

The relationship between forces and motion should be made clear. It should also be made clear that both light and vibrations from sound sources travel from the source to a detector. Work on the Earth's place in the solar system should be related to pupils' knowledge about light.

Pupils should be taught:

1. Electricity

simple circuits

a that a complete circuit, including a battery or power supply, is needed to make electrical devices work;

b how switches can be used to control electrical devices;

c ways of varying the current in a circuit to make bulbs brighter or dimmer;

d how to represent series circuits by drawings and diagrams, and how to construct series circuits on the basis of drawings and diagrams.

2. Forces and motion

types of force

a that there are forces of attraction and repulsion between magnets, and forces of attraction between magnets and magnetic materials;

b that objects have weight because of the gravitational attraction between them and the Earth;

c about friction, including air resistance, as a force which slows moving objects;

d that when springs and elastic bands are stretched they exert a force on whatever is stretching them;

e that when springs are compressed they exert a force on whatever is compressing them;

balanced and unbalanced forces

f that forces act in particular directions;

g that forces acting on an object can balance, *eg in a tug of war, on a floating object*, and that when this happens an object at rest stays still;

h that unbalanced forces can make things speed up, *eg an apple being dropped*, slow down, *eg a shoe sliding across the floor*, or change direction, *eg a ball being hit by a bat*.

Pupils should be taught:

3. Light and sound

everyday effects of light

a that light travels from a source;

b that light cannot pass through some materials, and that this leads to the formation of shadows;

c that light is reflected from surfaces, *eg mirrors, polished metals*;

seeing

d that we see light sources, *eg light bulbs, candles*, because light from them enters our eyes;

vibration and sound

e that sounds are made when objects, *eg strings on musical instruments*, vibrate but that vibrations are not always directly visible;

f that the pitch and loudness of sounds produced by some vibrating objects, *eg a drum skin, a plucked string*, can be changed;

g that vibrations from sound sources can travel through a variety of materials, *eg metals, wood, glass, air*, to the ear.

4. The Earth and beyond

the Sun, Earth and Moon

a that the Sun, Earth and Moon are approximately spherical;

periodic changes

b that the position of the Sun appears to change during the day, and how shadows change as this happens;

c that the Earth spins around its own axis, and how day and night are related to this spin;

d that the Earth orbits the Sun once each year, and that the Moon takes approximately 28 days to orbit the Earth.

ATTAINMENT TARGETS

LEVEL DESCRIPTIONS

The following level descriptions describe the types and range of performance that pupils working at a particular level should characteristically demonstrate. In deciding on a pupil's level of attainment at the end of a key stage, teachers should judge which description best fits the pupil's performance. Each description should be considered in conjunction with the descriptions for adjacent levels.

By the end of Key Stage 1, the performance of the great majority of pupils should be within the range of Levels 1 to 3, by the end of Key Stage 2 it should be within the range 2 to 5 and by the end of Key Stage 3 within the range 3 to 7.

■ Level 1

Pupils describe simple features of objects, living things and events they observe, communicating their findings in simple ways, such as by talking about their work or through drawings or simple charts.

■ Level 2

Pupils respond to suggestions of how to find things out and, with help, make their own suggestions. They use simple equipment provided and make observations related to their task. They compare objects, living things and events they observe. They describe their observations and record them using simple tables where it is appropriate to do so. They say whether what happened was what they expected.

■ Level 3

Pupils respond to suggestions, put forward their own ideas and, where appropriate, make simple predictions. They make relevant observations and measure quantities, such as length or mass, using a range of simple equipment. With some help they carry out a fair test, recognising and explaining why it is fair. They record their observations in a variety of ways. They provide explanations for observations and, where they occur, for simple patterns in recorded measurements. They say what they have found out from their work.

■ Level 4

Pupils recognise the need for fair tests, describing, or showing in the way they perform their task, how to vary one factor whilst keeping others the same. Where appropriate, they make predictions. They select suitable equipment to use and make a series of observations and measurements that are adequate for the task. They present their observations and measurements clearly, using tables and bar charts. They begin to plot points to form simple graphs and use these graphs to point out and interpret patterns or trends in their data. They take account of these patterns when they draw conclusions, and begin to relate their conclusions to scientific knowledge and understanding.

■ Level 5

Pupils identify the key factors they need to consider in contexts that involve only a few factors. Where appropriate, they make predictions based on their scientific knowledge and understanding. They select apparatus for a range of tasks and use it with care. They make a series of observations or measurements with precision appropriate to the task. They begin to repeat observations and measurements and to offer simple explanations for any differences they encounter. They record observations and measurements systematically and present data as line graphs. They draw conclusions that are consistent with the evidence and begin to relate these to scientific knowledge and understanding.

■ Level 6

Pupils use scientific knowledge and understanding to identify the key factors they need to consider and, where appropriate, to make predictions. They make observations and measure with precision a variety of quantities, using instruments with fine divisions. They make enough measurements and observations for the task. They choose scales for graphs that enable them to show appropriate data effectively. They identify measurements and observations that do not fit the main pattern or trend shown. They draw conclusions that are consistent with the evidence and explain these using scientific knowledge and understanding.

Science

Experimental
and
Investigative
Science

Level
Descriptions

Page 52

Level 1

Pupils recognise and name external parts of the body, using words such as head or arm, and of plants, using words such as leaf or flower. They observe and describe a range of animals and plants in terms of features such as colour of coat, or size of leaf. They recognise and identify a range of common animals, using terms such as fly, goldfish or robin.

Level 2

Pupils use their knowledge about living things to describe basic conditions, such as a supply of food, water, air or light, that animals and plants need in order to survive. They recognise that living things grow and reproduce. They sort living things into groups, using simple features. They describe the basis for their groupings in terms such as number of legs or shape of leaf. They recognise that different living things are found in different places, such as ponds or woods.

Level 3

Pupils use their knowledge of basic life processes, such as growth or reproduction, when they describe differences between living and non-living things. They provide simple explanations for changes in living things, such as diet affecting the health of humans or other animals, or lack of light or water altering plant growth. They identify ways in which an animal is suited to its environment, such as a fish having fins to help it swim.

Level 4

Pupils demonstrate knowledge and understanding of aspects of life processes and living things drawn from the Key Stage 2 or Key Stage 3 programme of study. They use scientific names for some major organs of body systems, such as the circulatory system, and identify the position of these organs in the human body. They identify organs, such as petal, stamen or stigma, of different plants they observe. They use keys based on observable external features to help them to identify and group living things systematically. They recognise that feeding relationships exist between plants and animals in a habitat, and describe these relationships, using food chains and terms such as predator and prey.

Level 5

Pupils demonstrate an increasing knowledge and understanding of aspects of life processes and living things drawn from the Key Stage 2 or Key Stage 3 programme of study. They describe the main functions of some organs of the human body, such as the heart, and of the flowering plant, such as the petal, stamen or stigma. They explain how these functions are essential to the organism. They describe the main stages of the life cycles of humans and flowering plants and point out similarities. They recognise that there is a great variety of living things and understand the importance of classification. They explain that different organisms are found in different habitats because of differences in environmental factors, such as the availability of light or water.

Level 6

Pupils use knowledge and understanding drawn from the Key Stage 3 programme of study, to describe and explain life processes and features of living things. They use appropriate scientific terminology when they describe life processes, such as respiration or photosynthesis, in animals and plants. They distinguish between related processes, such as pollination or fertilisation. They describe simple cell structure and identify differences between cells, such as differences in structure between simple animal and plant cells. They describe some of the factors that cause variation between living things. They explain that the distribution and abundance of organisms in habitats are affected by environmental factors, such as the availability of light or water.

■ Level 1

Pupils know about a range of properties, such as texture or appearance, and they describe materials they observe in terms of these properties.

■ Level 2

Pupils identify a range of common materials and know about some of their properties. They describe similarities and differences between materials. They sort materials into groups and describe in everyday terms, such as shininess, hardness or smoothness, the basis for their groupings. They describe ways in which some materials are changed by heating or cooling or by processes such as bending or stretching.

■ Level 3

Pupils use their knowledge and understanding of materials when they describe a variety of ways of sorting them into groups according to their properties. They explain why some materials are particularly suitable for specific purposes, such as a metal for making electrical cables. They recognise that some changes, such as the freezing of water, can be reversed and some, such as the baking of clay, cannot, and they classify changes in this way.

■ Level 4

Pupils demonstrate knowledge and understanding of aspects of materials and their properties drawn from the Key Stage 2 or Key Stage 3 programme of study. They describe differences between the properties of different materials and explain how these differences are used to classify substances as solids, liquids and gases. They describe some methods, such as filtration, that are used to separate simple mixtures. They use scientific terms, such as evaporation or condensation, to describe changes. They use knowledge about some reversible and irreversible changes to make simple predictions about whether other changes are reversible or not.

■ Level 5

Pupils demonstrate an increasing knowledge and understanding of aspects of materials and their properties drawn from the Key Stage 2 or Key Stage 3 programme of study. They describe some metallic properties, such as good electrical conductivity, and use these properties to distinguish metals from other solids. They identify a range of contexts in which changes, such as evaporation or condensation, take place. They use knowledge about how a specific mixture, such as salt and water, or sand and water, can be separated to suggest ways in which other similar mixtures might be separated.

■ Level 6

Pupils use knowledge and understanding of the nature and behaviour of materials drawn from the Key Stage 3 programme of study, to describe chemical and physical changes and how new materials can be made. They recognise that matter is made up of particles, and describe differences between the arrangement and movement of particles in solids, liquids and gases. They identify and describe similarities between some chemical reactions, such as the reactions of acids with metals or the reactions of a variety of substances with oxygen. They use word equations to summarise simple reactions. They relate changes of state to energy transfers, in contexts such as the formation of igneous rocks.

■ Level 1

Pupils describe the changes in light, sound or movement, which result from actions such as switching on a simple electrical circuit, or pushing and pulling objects. They recognise that sound and light come from a variety of sources and name some of these sources.

■ Level 2

Pupils know about a range of physical phenomena and recognise and describe similarities and differences associated with them. They compare the way in which devices, such as bulbs, work in different electrical circuits. They compare the effects of similar phenomena, such as the brightness or colour of lights, or the loudness or pitch of sounds. They compare the movement of different objects in terms of speed or direction.

■ Level 3

Pupils use their knowledge and understanding to link cause and effect in simple explanations of physical phenomena, such as a bulb failing to light because of a break in an electrical circuit, or the direction or speed of movement of an object changing because of a force applied to it. They begin to make simple generalisations about physical phenomena, such as explaining that sounds they hear become fainter the further they are from the source.

■ Level 4

Pupils demonstrate knowledge and understanding of aspects of physical processes drawn from the Key Stage 2 or Key Stage 3 programme of study. They describe and explain physical phenomena, such as how a particular device in an electrical circuit may be switched on or off, or how the apparent position of the Sun changes over the course of a day. They make generalisations about physical phenomena, such as motion being affected by forces, including gravitational attraction, magnetic attraction and friction, or sounds being heard through a variety of materials. They use the idea that light travels to explain phenomena such as the formation of shadows.

■ Level 5

Pupils demonstrate an increasing knowledge and understanding of aspects of physical processes drawn from the Key Stage 2 or Key Stage 3 programme of study. They begin to apply ideas about physical processes to suggest a variety of ways to make changes, such as altering the current in a circuit or altering the pitch or loudness of a sound. They begin to use some abstract ideas in descriptions, such as forces being balanced when an object is stationary, or objects being seen when light from them enters the eye. They use models to explain effects that are caused by the movement of the Earth, such as the length of a day or year.

■ Level 6

Pupils demonstrate understanding of how to apply some abstract ideas about physical processes drawn from the Key Stage 3 programme of study. They use abstract ideas in descriptions and explanations, such as electric current being a flow of charge, the sum of several forces determining changes in the direction or the speed of movement of an object, or wind and waves being energy resources available for use. They recognise that many physical concepts, such as the transfer of energy by light, sound or electricity, or the refraction and dispersion of light, apply in a variety of contexts, and describe some of these. They recognise that a number of factors may have to be considered when phenomena, such as the relative brightness of planets and stars, are explained.

Science

Physical
Processes

Level
Descriptions

Page 55

PROGRAMMES OF STUDY

COMMON REQUIREMENTS

Access

The programme of study for each key stage* should be taught to the great majority of pupils in the key stage, in ways appropriate to their abilities.

For the small number of pupils who may need the provision, material may be selected from earlier or later key stages where this is necessary to enable individual pupils to progress and demonstrate achievement. Such material should be presented in contexts suitable to the pupil's age.

Appropriate provision should be made for pupils who need to use:

- means of communication other than speech, including computers, technological aids, signing, symbols or lip-reading;

- non-sighted methods of reading, such as Braille, or non-visual or non-aural ways of acquiring information;

- technological aids in practical and written work;

- aids or adapted equipment to allow access to practical activities within and beyond school.

    Judgements made in relation to the level descriptions should allow for the provision above, where appropriate.

Use of language

Pupils should be taught to express themselves clearly in both speech and writing and to develop their reading skills. They should be taught to use grammatically correct sentences and to spell and punctuate accurately in order to communicate effectively in written English or, when the medium is Welsh, in written Welsh.

Information technology

Pupils should be given opportunities, where appropriate, to develop and apply their information technology (IT) capability in their study of design & technology.

The Curriculum Cymreig

In Wales, pupils should be given opportunities, where appropriate, in their study of design & technology to develop and apply their knowledge and understanding of the cultural, economic, environmental, historical and linguistic characteristics of Wales.

Referencing

The numbers and letters throughout the programmes of study are for referencing purposes only and do not necessarily indicate a particular teaching sequence or hierarchy of knowledge, understanding and skills.

Examples

Examples printed in italics are non-statutory.

---

* In Wales, there are no statutory requirements for design & technology at Key Stage 4.

> Pupils should be taught to develop their design & technology capability through combining their **Designing** and **Making skills** (paragraphs 3 and 4) with **Knowledge and understanding** (paragraph 5) in order to design and make products.

Design & Technology

Key Stage 1

1. Pupils should be given opportunities to develop their design & technology capability through:

  a assignments in which they design and make products;

  b focused practical tasks in which they develop and practise particular skills and knowledge;

  c activities in which they investigate, disassemble and evaluate simple products.

2. Pupils should be given opportunities to:

  a work with a range of materials and components, including sheet materials, items that can be assembled to make products, *eg reclaimed material*, textiles, food and construction kits;

  b investigate how the working characteristics of materials can be changed to suit different purposes;

  c apply skills, knowledge and understanding from the programmes of study of other subjects, where appropriate, including art, mathematics and science.

Pupils should be taught to:

3. Designing skills

  a draw on their own experience to help generate ideas;

  b clarify their ideas through discussion;

  c develop their ideas through shaping, assembling and rearranging materials and components;

  d develop and communicate their design ideas by making freehand drawings, and by modelling their ideas in other ways, *eg by using actual materials and components with temporary fixings*;

  e make suggestions about how to proceed;

  f consider their design ideas as these develop, and identify strengths and weaknesses.

4. Making skills

  a select materials, tools and techniques;

  b measure, mark out, cut and shape a range of materials;

  c assemble, join and combine materials and components;

  d apply simple finishing techniques, *eg painting*;

  e make suggestions about how to proceed;

  f evaluate their products as these are developed, identifying strengths and weaknesses.

Pupils should be taught:

■ 5. Knowledge and understanding

mechanisms

a to use simple mechanisms, including wheels and axles, and joints that allow movement;

structures

b how to make their structures more stable and withstand greater loads;

products and applications

c to investigate and disassemble simple products in order to learn how they function;

d to relate the ways things work to their intended purpose, how materials and components have been used, people's needs, and what users say about them;

quality

e that the quality of a product depends on how well it is made and how well it meets its purpose;

health and safety

f simple knowledge and understanding of health and safety, as consumers and when working with materials and components, including:

- considering the hazards and risks in their activities;
- following simple instructions to control risk to themselves;

vocabulary

g to use the appropriate vocabulary for naming and describing the equipment, materials and components they use.

Pupils should be taught to develop their design & technology capability through combining their **Designing** and **Making skills** (paragraphs 3 and 4) with **Knowledge and understanding** (paragraph 5) in order to design and make products.

1. Pupils should be given opportunities to develop their design & technology capability through:

a assignments in which they design and make products;

b focused practical tasks in which they develop and practise particular skills and knowledge;

c activities in which they investigate, disassemble and evaluate simple products.

2. Pupils should be given opportunities to:

a work with a range of materials and components, including stiff and flexible sheet materials, materials that are suitable for making frameworks, mouldable materials, textiles, food, electrical and mechanical components and construction kits;

b work independently and in teams;

c apply skills, knowledge and understanding from the programmes of study of other subjects, where appropriate, including art, mathematics and science.

Pupils should be taught to:

3. Designing skills

a use information sources to help in their designing;

b generate ideas, considering the users and purposes for which they are designing;

c clarify their ideas, develop criteria for their designs and suggest ways forward;

d consider appearance, function, safety and reliability when developing proposals;

e explore, develop and communicate aspects of their design proposals by modelling their ideas in a variety of ways;

f develop a clear idea of what has to be done, proposing a sequence of actions, and suggesting alternative methods of proceeding if things go wrong;

g evaluate their design ideas as these develop, bearing in mind the users and the purposes for which the product is intended, and indicate ways of improving their ideas.

4. Making skills

a select appropriate materials, tools and techniques;

b measure, mark out, cut and shape a range of materials, using additional tools, equipment and techniques;

c join and combine materials and components accurately in temporary and permanent ways;

Pupils should be taught to:

d apply additional finishing techniques, *eg cladding in paper or card*, appropriate to the materials being used and the purpose of the product;

e develop a clear idea of what has to be done, planning how to use materials, equipment and processes, and suggesting alternative methods of making if first attempts fail;

f evaluate their products, identifying strengths and weaknesses, and carrying out appropriate tests, *eg on strength, user reaction, function*;

g implement improvements they have identified.

Pupils should be taught:

5. Knowledge and understanding

materials and components

a how the working characteristics of materials relate to the ways materials are used;

b how materials can be combined and mixed in order to create more useful properties, *eg incorporating new materials in a structure to strengthen it, combining different ingredients in a salad to produce a variety of textures*;

control

c how simple mechanisms can be used to produce different types of movement;

d how electrical circuits, including those with simple switches, can be used to achieve functional results;

structures

e how structures can fail when loaded, and techniques for reinforcing and strengthening them;

products and applications

f to investigate, disassemble and evaluate simple products and applications, including those with mechanical and electrical components, in order to learn how they function;

g to relate the way things work to their intended purpose, how materials and components have been used, people's needs, and what users say about them;

quality

h to distinguish between how well a product has been made and how well it has been designed;

i to consider the effectiveness of a product, including the extent to which it meets a clear need, is fit for purpose, and uses resources appropriately;

health and safety

j further knowledge and understanding of health and safety as designers, makers and consumers, including:

- recognising hazards to themselves and to others in a range of products, activities and environments;
- assessing risks to themselves and to others;
- taking action to control these risks;

vocabulary

k to use the appropriate vocabulary for naming and describing the equipment, materials and components, and processes they use.

ATTAINMENT TARGETS

LEVEL DESCRIPTIONS

The following level descriptions describe the types and range of performance that pupils working at a particular level should characteristically demonstrate. In deciding on a pupil's level of attainment at the end of a key stage, teachers should judge which description best fits the pupil's performance. Each description should be considered in conjunction with the descriptions for adjacent levels.

By the end of Key Stage 1, the performance of the great majority of pupils should be within the range of Levels 1 to 3, by the end of Key Stage 2 it should be within the range 2 to 5 and by the end of Key Stage 3 within the range 3 to 7.

Level 1

When designing and making, pupils generate ideas through shaping, assembling and rearranging materials and components. They recognise the simple features of familiar products and, when prompted, relate them to their own ideas. They use pictures and words to convey what they want to do.

Level 2

When designing and making, pupils use their experiences of using materials, techniques and products to help generate ideas. They use models and pictures to develop and communicate their designs. They reflect on their ideas and suggest improvements.

Level 3

When designing and making, pupils generate ideas, recognising that their designs will have to satisfy conflicting requirements. They make realistic suggestions about how they can achieve their intentions and suggest more ideas when asked. They draw on their knowledge and understanding of the appropriate programme of study to help them generate ideas. Labelled sketches are used to show the details of their designs.

Level 4

When designing and making, pupils gather information independently, and use it to help generate a number of ideas. They recognise that users have views and preferences, and are beginning to take them into account. They evaluate their work as it develops, bearing in mind the purposes for which it is intended. They illustrate alternatives using sketches and models and make choices between them, showing an awareness of constraints.

Level 5

When designing and making, pupils generate ideas that draw upon external sources and their understanding of the characteristics of familiar products. They clarify their ideas through discussion, drawing and modelling, using their knowledge and understanding of the appropriate programme of study to help them. Pupils evaluate ideas, showing understanding of the situations in which their designs will have to function, and awareness of resources as a constraint.

Level 6

When designing and making, pupils generate ideas that draw on a wider range of sources of information, including those not immediately related to the task, and an understanding of the form and function of familiar products. They develop criteria for their designs, which take into account appearance, function, safety, reliability and the users and purposes for which they are intended, and use these to formulate a design proposal. They make preliminary models to explore and test their design thinking, and use formal drawing methods to communicate their intentions.

Design
&
Technology

Designing

Level
Descriptions

Page 64

Level 1

When designing and making, pupils explain what they are making and which materials they are using. They select from a narrow range of materials and use given techniques and tools to shape, assemble and join them.

Level 2

When designing and making, pupils select from a range of materials, tools and techniques, explaining their choices. They manipulate tools safely and assemble and join materials in a variety of ways. They make judgements about the outcomes of their work.

Level 3

When designing and making, pupils think ahead about the order of their work, choosing tools, materials and techniques more purposefully. They use tools with some accuracy and use simple finishing techniques to improve their products. They cut and shape materials and components, with some precision, to help assembly. Their products are similar to their original intentions and, where changes have been made, they are identified.

Level 4

When designing and making, pupils produce step-by-step plans that identify the main stages in making, and list the tools, materials and processes needed. They measure, mark out and cut simple forms in a variety of materials and join them using a range of techniques. They show increasing accuracy, paying attention to quality of finish and function. They identify what is, and what is not, working well in their products.

Level 5

When designing and making, pupils work from plans they have produced, modifying them in the light of difficulties. They use a range of tools, materials and processes safely with increasing precision and control. They use measuring and checking procedures as their work develops, and modify their approach if first attempts fail. They evaluate their products by comparing them with their design intentions and suggest ways of improving them.

Level 6

When designing and making, pupils produce plans that outline the implications of their design decisions, and suggest alternative methods of proceeding if first attempts should fail. They are becoming increasingly skilful in the use of the techniques and processes identified in the Key Stage 3 Programme of Study, and use tools and equipment to work materials precisely. They evaluate their products in use and identify ways of improving them.

PROGRAMMES OF STUDY

COMMON REQUIREMENTS

■ Access

The programme of study for each key stage* should be taught to the great majority of pupils in the key stage, in ways appropriate to their abilities.

For the small number of pupils who may need the provision, material may be selected from earlier or later key stages where this is necessary to enable individual pupils to progress and demonstrate achievement. Such material should be presented in contexts suitable to the pupil's age.

Appropriate provision should be made for pupils who need to use:

- means of communication other than speech, including computers, technological aids, signing, symbols or lip-reading;

- non-sighted methods of reading, such as Braille, or non-visual or non-aural ways of acquiring information;

- technological aids in practical and written work;

- aids or adapted equipment to allow access to practical activities within and beyond school.

   Judgements made in relation to the level descriptions should allow for the provision above, where appropriate.

■ Use of language

Pupils should be taught to express themselves clearly in both speech and writing and to develop their reading skills. They should be taught to use grammatically correct sentences and to spell and punctuate accurately in order to communicate effectively in written English or, when the medium is Welsh, in written Welsh.

■ Information technology capability

Information technology (IT) capability is characterised by an ability to use effectively IT tools and information sources to analyse, process and present information, and to model, measure and control external events. This involves:

- using information sources and IT tools to solve problems;

- using IT tools and information sources, such as computer systems and software packages, to support learning in a variety of contexts;

- understanding the implications of IT for working life and society.

Pupils should be given opportunities, where appropriate, to develop and apply their IT capability in their study of National Curriculum subjects.

■ The Curriculum Cymreig

In Wales, pupils should be given opportunities, where appropriate, in their study of information technology to develop and apply their knowledge and understanding of the cultural, economic, environmental, historical and linguistic characteristics of Wales.

■ Referencing

The numbers and letters throughout the programmes of study are for referencing purposes only and do not necessarily indicate a particular teaching sequence or hierarchy of knowledge, understanding and skills.

---

* In Wales, there are no statutory requirements for IT at Key Stage 4.

Pupils should be taught to use IT equipment and software confidently and purposefully to communicate and handle information, and to support their problem solving, recording and expressive work.

■ 1. Pupils should be given opportunities to:

a use a variety of IT equipment and software, including microcomputers and various keyboards, to carry out a variety of functions in a range of contexts;

b explore the use of computer systems and control technology in everyday life;

c examine and discuss their experiences of IT, and look at the use of IT in the outside world.

Pupils should be taught to:

■ 2. Communicating and handling information

a generate and communicate their ideas in different forms, using text, tables, pictures and sound;

b enter and store information;

c retrieve, process and display information that has been stored.

■ 3. Controlling and modelling

a recognise that control is integral to many everyday devices;

b give direct signals or commands that produce a variety of outcomes, and describe the effects of their actions;

c use IT-based models or simulations to explore aspects of real and imaginary situations.

Pupils should be taught to extend the range of IT tools that they use for communication, investigation and control; become discerning in their use of IT; select information, sources and media for their suitability for purpose; and assess the value of IT in their working practices.

■ 1. Pupils should be given opportunities to:

a use IT to explore and solve problems in the context of work across a variety of subjects;

b use IT to further their understanding of information that they have retrieved and processed;

c discuss their experiences of using IT and assess its value in their working practices;

d investigate parallels with the use of IT in the wider world, consider the effects of such uses, and compare them with other methods.

Pupils should be taught to:

■ 2. Communicating and handling information

a use IT equipment and software to communicate ideas and information in a variety of forms, incorporating text, graphs, pictures and sound, as appropriate, showing sensitivity to the needs of their audience;

b use IT equipment and software to organise, reorganise and analyse ideas and information;

c select suitable information and media, and classify and prepare information for processing with IT, checking for accuracy;

d interpret, analyse and check the plausibility of information held on IT systems, and select the elements required for particular purposes, considering the consequences of any errors.

■ 3. Controlling, monitoring and modelling

a create, test, modify and store sequences of instructions to control events;

b use IT equipment and software to monitor external events;

c explore the effect of changing variables in simulations and similar packages, to ask and answer questions of the 'What would happen if...?' type;

d recognise patterns and relationships in the results obtained from IT-based models or simulations, predicting the outcomes of different decisions that could be made.

Information Technology

Key Stage 2

The following level descriptions describe the types and range of performance that pupils working at a particular level should characteristically demonstrate. In deciding on a pupil's level of attainment at the end of a key stage, teachers should judge which description best fits the pupil's performance. Each description should be considered in conjunction with the descriptions for adjacent levels.

By the end of Key Stage 1, the performance of the great majority of pupils should be within the range of Levels 1 to 3, by the end of Key Stage 2 it should be within the range 2 to 5 and by the end of Key Stage 3 within the range 3 to 7.

■ Level 1

Pupils use IT to assemble text and symbols to help them communicate ideas. They explore information held on IT systems, showing an awareness that information exists in a variety of forms. They recognise that many everyday devices respond to signals and commands, and that they can select options when using such devices to produce different outcomes.

■ Level 2

Pupils use IT to help them generate and communicate ideas in different forms, such as text, tables, pictures and sound. With some support, they retrieve and store work. They use IT to sort and classify information and to present their findings. Pupils control devices purposefully and describe the effects of their actions. They use IT-based models or simulations to investigate options as they explore aspects of real and imaginary situations.

■ Level 3

Pupils use IT to generate, amend, organise and present ideas. They use IT to save data and to access stored information, following straightforward lines of enquiry. They understand how to control equipment to achieve specific outcomes by giving a series of instructions. They use IT-based models or simulations to help them make decisions, and are aware of the consequences of their choices. They describe their use of IT, and its use in the outside world.

■ Level 4

Pupils use IT to combine different forms of information, and show an awareness of audience. They add to, amend and interrogate information that has been stored. They understand the need for care in framing questions when collecting, accessing and interrogating information. Pupils interpret their findings, question plausibility and recognise that poor quality information yields unreliable results. Pupils use IT systems to control events in a predetermined manner, to sense physical data and to display it. They use IT-based models and simulations to explore patterns and relationships, and make simple predictions about the consequences of their decision making. They compare their use of IT with other methods.

■ Level 5

Pupils use IT to organise, refine and present information in different forms and styles for specific purposes and audiences. They select the information needed for different purposes, check its accuracy and organise and prepare it in a form suitable for processing using IT. They create sets of instructions to control events, and are becoming sensitive to the need for precision in framing and sequencing instructions. They explore the effects of changing the variables in a computer model. They communicate their knowledge and experience of using IT and assess its use in their working practices.

■ Level 6

Pupils develop and refine work, using information from a range of sources, and demonstrating a clear sense of audience and purpose in their presentation. Where necessary, they use complex lines of enquiry to test hypotheses. They develop, trial and refine sets of instructions to control events, demonstrating an awareness of the notions of efficiency and economy in framing these instructions. They understand how IT devices can be used to monitor and measure external events, using sensors. Pupils use computer models of increasing complexity, vary the rules within them, and assess the validity of these models by comparing their behaviour with other data. They discuss the wider impact of IT on society.

COMMON REQUIREMENTS

■ Access

The programme of study for each key stage should be taught to the great majority of pupils in the key stage, in ways appropriate to their abilities.

For the small number of pupils who may need the provision, material may be selected from earlier or later key stages where this is necessary to enable individual pupils to progress and demonstrate achievement. Such material should be presented in contexts suitable to the pupil's age.

Appropriate provision should be made for pupils who need to use:

- means of communication other than speech, including computers, technological aids, signing, symbols or lip-reading;

- non-sighted methods of reading, such as Braille, or non-visual or non-aural ways of acquiring information;

- technological aids in practical and written work;

- aids or adapted equipment to allow access to practical activities within and beyond school.

   Judgements made in relation to the level descriptions should allow for the provision above, where appropriate.

■ Use of language

Pupils should be taught to express themselves clearly in both speech and writing and to develop their reading skills. They should be taught to use grammatically correct sentences and to spell and punctuate accurately in order to communicate effectively in written English.

■ Information technology

Pupils should be given opportunities, where appropriate, to develop and apply their information technology (IT) capability in their study of history.

■ Referencing

The numbers and letters throughout the programmes of study are for referencing purposes only and do not necessarily indicate a particular teaching sequence or hierarchy of knowledge, understanding and skills.

■ Examples

Examples printed in italics are non-statutory.

Pupils should be given opportunities to develop an awareness of the past and of the ways in which it was different from the present. They should be helped to set their study of the past in a chronological framework and to understand some of the ways in which we find out about the past.

The Areas of Study and the Key Elements, outlined below, should be taught together.

AREAS OF STUDY

■ **1.** Pupils should be taught about the everyday life, work, leisure and culture of men, women and children in the past, *eg clothes, diet, everyday objects, houses, shops and other buildings, jobs, transport, entertainment*. In progressing from familiar situations to those more distant in time and place, pupils should be given opportunities to investigate:

    a changes in their own lives and those of their family or adults around them;

    b aspects of the way of life of people in Britain in the past beyond living memory.

■ **2.** Pupils should be taught about the lives of different kinds of famous men and women, including personalities drawn from British history, *eg rulers, saints, artists, engineers, explorers, inventors, pioneers*.

■ **3.** Pupils should be taught about past events of different types, including events from the history of Britain, *eg notable local and national events, events in other countries, events that have been remembered and commemorated by succeeding generations, such as centenaries, religious festivals, anniversaries, the Gunpowder Plot, the Olympic Games*.

KEY ELEMENTS

The Key Elements are closely related and should be developed through the Areas of Study, as appropriate. Not all the Key Elements need to be developed in each Area of Study.

Pupils should be taught:

■ **1. Chronology**

    a to sequence events and objects, in order to develop a sense of chronology;

    b to use common words and phrases relating to the passing of time, *eg old, new, before, after, long ago, days of the week, months, years.*

■ **2. Range and depth of historical knowledge and understanding**

    a about aspects of the past through stories from different periods and cultures, including stories and eyewitness accounts of historical events;

    b to recognise why people did things, why events happened and what happened as a result;

    c to identify differences between ways of life at different times.

■ **3. Interpretations of history**

    a to identify different ways in which the past is represented, *eg pictures, written accounts, films, television programmes, plays, songs, reproductions of objects, museum displays.*

■ **4. Historical enquiry**

    a how to find out about aspects of the past from a range of sources of information, including artefacts, pictures and photographs, adults talking about their own past, written sources, and buildings and sites;

    b to ask and answer questions about the past.

■ **5. Organisation and communication**

    a to communicate their awareness and understanding of history in a variety of ways.

Pupils should be taught about important episodes and developments in Britain's past, from Roman to modern times, about ancient civilisations and the history of other parts of the world. They should be helped to develop a chronological framework by making links across the different study units. They should have opportunities to investigate local history and to learn about the past from a range of sources of information.

The Study Units and the Key Elements, outlined below, should be taught together.

STUDY UNITS

History Key Stage 2

Pupils should be taught SIX Study Units.

■ **1. Romans, Anglo-Saxons and Vikings in Britain**
The history of the British Isles from 55 BC to the early eleventh century, and the ways in which British society was shaped by different peoples. Pupils should be given opportunities to study, in greater depth, ONE of the Romans, the Anglo-Saxons, or the Vikings.

■ **2. Life in Tudor times**
Some of the major events and personalities, including monarchs, and the way of life of people at different levels of society in Tudor times.

■ **3a. Victorian Britain**
The lives of men, women and children at different levels of society, in Britain, and the ways in which they were affected by changes in industry and transport.

──────────── OR ────────────

■ **3b. Britain since 1930**
The lives of men, women and children at different levels of society, in Britain, and the ways in which they were affected by the Second World War and changes in technology and transport.

■ **4. Ancient Greece**
The way of life, beliefs and achievements of the ancient Greeks, and the legacy of ancient Greek civilisation to the modern world.

■ **5. Local history**
An aspect of local history.

■ **6. A past non-European society**
The key features of a past non-European society.

Details of each Study Unit are given on pages 6–9.

■ **7.** Across the key stage, pupils should be given opportunities to study:

    a aspects of the past in outline and in depth;

    b aspects of the histories of England, Ireland, Scotland and Wales; where appropriate, the history of Britain should be set in its European and world context;

    c history from a variety of perspectives – political; economic, technological and scientific; social; religious; cultural and aesthetic.

KEY ELEMENTS

The Key Elements are closely related and should be developed through the Study Units, as appropriate. Not all the Key Elements need to be developed in each Study Unit.

Pupils should be taught:

■ **1. Chronology**

    a to place the events, people and changes in the periods studied within a chronological framework;

    b to use dates and terms relating to the passing of time, including ancient, modern, BC, AD, century and decade, and terms that define different periods, *eg Tudor, Victorian.*

■ **2. Range and depth of historical knowledge and understanding**

    a about characteristic features of particular periods and societies, including the ideas, beliefs and attitudes of people in the past, and the experiences of men and women; and about the social, cultural, religious and ethnic diversity of the societies studied;

    b to describe and identify reasons for and results of historical events, situations, and changes in the periods studied;

    c to describe and make links between the main events, situations and changes both within and across periods.

History

Key Stage 2

■ **3. Interpretations of history**

    a to identify and give reasons for different ways in which the past is represented and interpreted.

■ **4. Historical enquiry**

    a how to find out about aspects of the periods studied, from a range of sources of information, including documents and printed sources, artefacts, pictures and photographs, music, and buildings and sites;

    b to ask and answer questions, and to select and record information relevant to a topic.

■ **5. Organisation and communication**

    a to recall, select and organise historical information, including dates and terms;

    b the terms necessary to describe the periods and topics studied, including court, monarch, parliament, nation, civilisations, invasion, conquest, settlement, conversion, slavery, trade, industry, law;

    c to communicate their knowledge and understanding of history in a variety of ways, including structured narratives and descriptions.

Study Unit 1: Romans, Anglo-Saxons, and Vikings in Britain

Pupils should be taught about the history of the British Isles from 55 BC to the early eleventh century, and the ways in which British society was shaped by different peoples. They should be given opportunities to study, in greater depth, ONE of the Romans, the Anglo-Saxons, or the Vikings.

■ **1.** Pupils should be taught **in outline** about the following:

- **a** the Roman conquest and occupation of Britain;

- **b** the arrival and settlement of the Anglo-Saxons;

- **c** Viking raids and settlements.

■ **2.** They should be taught **in greater depth** about ONE of the following:

a. Romans

- ■ the Roman conquest and its impact on Britain, *eg Boudicca and resistance to Roman rule, the extent to which life in Celtic Britain was influenced by Roman rule and settlement, the end of imperial rule*;

- ■ everyday life, *eg houses and home life, work, religion*;

- ■ the legacy of Roman rule, *eg place names and settlement patterns, Roman remains, including artefacts, roads and buildings.*

———————— OR ————————

b. Anglo-Saxons

- ■ the arrival and settlement of the Anglo-Saxons and their impact on England, *eg early settlement, the conversion of the Anglo-Saxons to Christianity, King Alfred and Anglo-Saxon resistance to the Vikings*;

- ■ everyday life, *eg houses and home life, work, religion*;

- ■ the legacy of settlement, *eg place names and settlement patterns, myths and legends, Anglo-Saxon remains, including artefacts and buildings.*

———————— OR ————————

c. Vikings

- ■ Viking raids and settlement and their impact on the British Isles, *eg their settlement in different parts of the British Isles, King Alfred and Anglo-Saxon resistance to the Vikings*;

- ■ everyday life, *eg houses and home life, work, religion*;

- ■ the legacy of settlement, *eg place names and settlement patterns, myths and legends, Viking remains, including artefacts and buildings.*

Study Unit 2: Life in Tudor times

Pupils should be taught about some of the major events and personalities, including monarchs, and the way of life of people at different levels of society in Tudor times:

Major events and personalities

a Henry VIII and the break with Rome, *eg the divorce question, the dissolution of the monasteries*;

b exploration overseas, *eg the voyages of Sebastian and John Cabot, Francis Drake and Walter Raleigh*;

c Elizabeth I and the Armada (1588);

The ways of life of people at different levels of society

d Court life, *eg the progresses of Elizabeth I, the role of a personality such as Thomas More or the Earl of Essex*;

e ways of life in town and country, *eg home life, work and leisure, health, trade*;

f arts and architecture, including Shakespeare, *eg Elizabethan theatres, music, paintings, town houses, manor houses, and country houses and their estates.*

Study Unit 3a: Victorian Britain

Pupils should be taught about the lives of men, women and children at different levels of society in Britain and the ways in which they were affected by changes in industry and transport:

Changes in industry and transport

a steam power, factories and mass production, *eg economic growth and the provision of jobs for men and women, the impact of mass production on living and working conditions*;

b the growth of railways, *eg the work of Robert Stephenson and Isambard Kingdom Brunel, the impact of railways on everyday life*;

The lives of people at different levels of society in town and country

c at work, *eg factory life, Lord Shaftesbury and factory reform, Florence Nightingale and nursing, domestic service, agriculture, the armed forces, the merchant marine, workhouses*;

d at home, *eg family life at different levels of society, Victoria and the royal family, the role of religion, public health and medicine*;

e at leisure, *eg music, sport, holidays, the Great Exhibition*;

f at school, *eg Sunday schools, voluntary schools, board schools, public schools.*

Study Unit 3b: Britain since 1930

Pupils should be taught about the lives of men, women and children at different levels of society in Britain and the ways in which they were affected by the Second World War and changes in technology and transport:

Changes in technology and transport

a changes in industry and transport, including the impact of new technologies, *eg motor cars, computers, space travel*;

Britons at war

b the impact of the Second World War on the people of Britain, *eg evacuation, the Blitz, the armed forces, rationing*;

The lives of people at different levels of society in different parts of Britain

c at home, *eg family life at different levels of society, housing conditions, diet and health, changes in the roles of men and women*;

d at work, *eg the Depression, changes in employment, automation, men and women at work, emigration and immigration*;

e at leisure, *eg radio, cinema and television, the Festival of Britain, sport, holidays*.

Study Unit 4: Ancient Greece

Pupils should be taught about the way of life, beliefs and achievements of the ancient Greeks and the legacy of ancient Greek civilisation to the modern world:

The ancient Greeks

a Athens and Sparta, *eg everyday life, citizens and slaves*;

b arts and architecture, *eg pottery, sculpture, theatres, temples, public buildings, and how these help us to find out about the ancient Greeks*;

c myths and legends of Greek gods and goddesses, heroes and heroines;

d relations with other peoples, *eg Persians, such as the stories of Marathon, Thermopylae and Salamis, the Greeks in Southern Italy, the campaigns of Alexander the Great, the influence on the Greeks of other civilisations, such as Egypt or Rome*;

The legacy of ancient Greek civilisation

e influence on the modern world, *eg politics, language, sport, architecture, science*.

Study Unit 5: Local history

Pupils should be taught about an aspect of local history. This should be ONE of the following:

a an aspect of the local community over a long period of time, *eg education, leisure, religion, population change, settlement and landscape, law and order, the treatment of the poor*;

————————————OR————————————

b an aspect of the local community during a short period of time or the local community's involvement in a particular event, *eg Viking York, the impact of the Norman Conquest on a local area, deserted medieval villages in an area, the local area during the Civil War, how the land was enclosed, the impact of the First World War on the locality*;

————————————OR————————————

c an aspect of the local community that illustrates developments taught in the study units, *eg local fortifications, the Romans, Anglo-Saxons or Vikings in the local area, life in the country house, child labour in the Industrial Revolution, new towns in the twentieth century*.

**History
Key Stage 2**

Study Unit 6: A past non-European society

Pupils should be taught about key features of a past non-European society chosen from the following list:

- Ancient Egypt;
- Mesopotamia, *eg Ancient Sumer or the Assyrian Empire*;
- the Indus Valley;
- the Maya;
- Benin;
- the Aztecs.

This unit should cover:

a key features, including the everyday lives of men and women;

b the use of archaeology in finding out about the people and society.

LEVEL DESCRIPTIONS

The following level descriptions describe the types and range of performance that pupils working at a particular level should characteristically demonstrate. In deciding on a pupil's level of attainment at the end of the key stage, teachers should judge which description best fits the pupil's performance. Each description should be considered in conjunction with the descriptions for adjacent levels.

By the end of Key Stage 1, the performance of the great majority of pupils should be within the range of Levels 1 to 3, by the end of Key Stage 2 it should be within the range 2 to 5 and by the end of Key Stage 3 within the range 3 to 7.

■ Level 1

Pupils recognise the distinction between present and past in their own and other people's lives. They show their emerging sense of chronology by sequencing a few events and objects, and by using everyday terms about the passing of time. They know and recount episodes from stories about the past. They are beginning to find answers to questions about the past from sources of information.

■ Level 2

Pupils show their developing sense of chronology by using terms concerned with the passing of time, by ordering events and objects, and by making distinctions between aspects of their own lives and past times. They demonstrate factual knowledge and understanding of aspects of the past beyond living memory, and of some of the main events and people they have studied. They are beginning to recognise that there are reasons why people in the past acted as they did. They are beginning to identify some of the different ways in which the past is represented. They answer questions about the past, from sources of information, on the basis of simple observations.

■ Level 3

Pupils show their understanding of chronology by their increasing awareness that the past can be divided into different periods of time, their recognition of some of the similarities and differences between these periods, and their use of dates and terms. They demonstrate factual knowledge and understanding of some of the main events, people and changes drawn from the appropriate programme of study. They are beginning to give a few reasons for, and results of, the main events and changes. They identify some of the different ways in which the past is represented. They find answers to questions about the past by using sources of information in ways that go beyond simple observations.

■ Level 4

Pupils demonstrate factual knowledge and understanding of aspects of the history of Britain and other countries, drawn from the Key Stage 2 or Key Stage 3 programme of study. They use this to describe the characteristic features of past societies and periods, and to identify changes within and across periods. They describe some of the main events, people and changes. They give some reasons for, and results of, the main events and changes. They show how some aspects of the past have been represented and interpreted in different ways. They are beginning to select and combine information from sources. They are beginning to produce structured work, making appropriate use of dates and terms.

■ Level 5

Pupils demonstrate an increasing depth of factual knowledge and understanding of aspects of the history of Britain and other countries drawn from the Key Stage 2 or Key Stage 3 programme of study. They use this to describe and to begin to make links between features of past societies and periods. They describe events, people and changes. They describe and make links between relevant reasons for, and results of, events and changes. They know that some events, people and changes have been interpreted in different ways and suggest possible reasons for this. Using their knowledge and understanding, pupils are beginning to evaluate sources of information and identify those that are useful for particular tasks. They select and organise information to produce structured work, making appropriate use of dates and terms.

■ Level 6

Pupils use their factual knowledge and understanding of the history of Britain and other countries drawn from the Key Stage 3 programme of study, to describe past societies and periods, and to make links between features within and across periods. They examine, and are beginning to analyse the reasons for, and results of, events and changes. Pupils describe, and are beginning to explain, different historical interpretations of events, people and changes. Using their knowledge and understanding, they identify and evaluate sources of information, which they use critically to reach and support conclusions. They select, organise and deploy relevant information to produce structured work, making appropriate use of dates and terms.

COMMON REQUIREMENTS

■ Access

The programme of study for each key stage should be taught to all or the great majority of pupils in the key stage, in ways appropriate to their abilities.

For the small number of pupils who may need the provision, material may be selected from earlier or later key stages where this is necessary to enable individual pupils to progress and demonstrate achievement. Such material should be presented in contexts suitable to the pupil's age.

Appropriate provision should be made for pupils who need to use:

- means of communication other than speech, including computers, technological aids, signing, symbols or lip-reading;

- non-sighted methods of reading, such as Braille, or non-visual or non-aural ways of acquiring information;

- technological aids in practical and written work;

- aids or adapted equipment to allow access to practical activities within and beyond school.

Judgements made in relation to the level descriptions should allow for the provision above, where appropriate.

■ Use of language

Pupils should be taught to express themselves clearly in both speech and writing and to develop their reading skills. They should be taught to use grammatically correct sentences and to spell and punctuate accurately in order to communicate effectively in written English.

■ Information technology

Pupils should be given opportunities, where appropriate, to develop and apply their information technology (IT) capability in their study of geography.

■ Referencing

The numbers and letters throughout the programmes of study are for referencing purposes only and do not necessarily indicate a particular teaching sequence or hierarchy of knowledge, understanding and skills.

■ Examples

Examples printed in italics are non-statutory.

**Geography
Key Stage 1**

■ **1.** Pupils should be given opportunities to:

  a investigate the physical and human features of their surroundings;

  b undertake studies that focus on geographical questions, *eg 'What / Where is it?', 'What is it like?', 'How did it get like this?',* and that are based on direct experience, practical activities and fieldwork in the locality of the school; studies should involve the development of skills, and the development of knowledge and understanding about places and themes;

  c become aware that the world extends beyond their own locality, both within and outside the United Kingdom, and that the places they study exist within this broader geographical context, *eg within a town, a region, a country.*

GEOGRAPHICAL SKILLS

■ **2.** In investigating places and a theme, pupils should be given opportunities to observe, question and record, and to communicate ideas and information.

■ **3.** Pupils should be taught to:

  a use geographical terms, *eg hill, river, road,* in exploring their surroundings;

  b undertake fieldwork activities in the locality of the school, *eg observing housing types, mapping the school playground;*

  c follow directions, including the terms up, down, on, under, behind, in front of, near, far, left, right, north, south, east, west;

  d make maps and plans of real and imaginary places, using pictures and symbols, *eg a pictorial map of a place featured in a story, a plan of their route from home to school;*

  e use globes, maps and plans at a variety of scales; the work should include identifying major geographical features, *eg seas, rivers, cities,* locating and naming on a map the constituent countries of the United Kingdom, marking on a map approximately where they live, and following a route;

  f use secondary sources, *eg pictures, photographs (including aerial photographs), books, videos, CD-ROM encyclopaedia,* to obtain geographical information.

PLACES

■ **4.** Two localities should be studied: the locality of the school and a locality, either in the United Kingdom or overseas, in which the physical and/or human features contrast with those in the locality of the school. The locality of the school is its immediate vicinity; it includes the school buildings and grounds and the surrounding area within easy access. The contrasting locality should be an area of similar size.

■ **5.** In these studies, pupils should be taught:

a about the main physical and human features, *eg rivers, hills, factories, shops,* that give the localities their character;

b how localities may be similar and how they may differ, *eg both areas may have farmland, but animals may be kept on the farms in one area, while in the other crops may be grown;*

c about the effects of weather on people and their surroundings, *eg the effect of seasonal variations in temperature on the clothes people wear;*

d how land and buildings, *eg farms, parks, factories, houses,* are used.

THEMATIC STUDY

■ **6.** The quality of the environment in any locality, either in the United Kingdom or overseas, should be investigated.

In this study, pupils should be taught:

a to express views on the attractive and unattractive features, *eg tidiness, noise,* of the environment concerned, *eg a play area, a street, a small area of woodland;*

b how that environment is changing, *eg increasing traffic;*

c how the quality of that environment can be sustained and improved, *eg creating cycle lanes, excluding cars from an area.*

**Geography
Key Stage 2**

■ **1.** Pupils should be given opportunities to:

    a investigate places and themes across a widening range of scales;

    b undertake studies that focus on geographical questions, *eg 'What/where is it?', 'What is it like?', 'How did it get like this?', 'How and why is it changing?'*, and that involve fieldwork and classroom activities; studies should involve the development of skills, and the development of knowledge and understanding about places and themes;

    c develop the ability to recognise patterns, *eg variations in rainfall between places, patterns of land use in a settlement*, and to apply their knowledge and understanding to explain them;

    d become aware of how places fit into a wider geographical context, *eg links within a town, a rural area, a region.*

GEOGRAPHICAL SKILLS

■ **2.** In investigating places and themes, pupils should be given opportunities to:

    a observe and ask questions about geographical features and issues;

    b collect and record evidence to answer the questions;

    c analyse the evidence, draw conclusions and communicate findings.

■ **3.** Pupils should be taught to:

    a use appropriate geographical vocabulary, *eg temperature, transport, industry, agriculture*, to describe and interpret their surroundings;

    b undertake fieldwork, including the use of instruments to make measurements, *eg rain gauges*, and appropriate techniques, *eg questionnaires*;

    c make plans and maps at a variety of scales, using symbols and keys, *eg drawing a sketch map of a housing estate*;

    d use and interpret globes, and maps and plans at a variety of scales; the work should include using co-ordinates and four-figure grid references, measuring direction and distance, following routes, using the contents pages and index of an atlas, and identifying the points of reference specified on Maps A, B and C (pages 7–9);

    e use secondary sources of evidence – pictures, photographs (including aerial photographs) and other sources, *eg television and radio programmes, books, newspapers, visitors to the school* – to inform their studies;

    f use IT to gain access to additional information sources and to assist in handling, classifying and presenting evidence, *eg recording fieldwork evidence on spreadsheets, using newspapers on CD-ROM, using word-processing and mapping packages.*

PLACES

■ **4.** Three localities should be studied. One study should focus on the locality of the school, which, at this key stage, should cover an area larger than the school's immediate vicinity. It will normally contain the homes of the majority of pupils in the school. The two contrasting localities should be similar in size to the locality of the school. One locality should be in the United Kingdom and the other in a country in Africa, Asia (excluding Japan), South America or Central America (including the Caribbean).

■ **5.** In these studies, pupils should be taught:

a about the main physical and human features, *eg cliffs, valleys, housing estates, reservoirs*, and environmental issues, *eg water pollution, proposals for a new supermarket*, that give the localities their character;

b how the localities may be similar and how they may differ, *eg two localities may both be in valleys, but one valley is narrow and steep-sided, while the other is wide and gently sloping*;

c how the features of the localities influence the nature and location of human activities within them, *eg roads following valleys, multi-storey car parks near city centres*;

d about recent or proposed changes in the localities, *eg closure of a corner shop*;

e how the localities are set within a broader geographical context, *eg within a town, a region, a country*, and are linked with other places, *eg through the supply of goods, movement of people*.

THEMATIC STUDIES

■ **6.** The four geographical themes below should be investigated. These may be studied separately, in combination with other themes, or as part of the studies of places. Whichever approach is followed, these studies should be set within the context of actual places and some should use topical examples. Taken together, the studies should involve work at a range of scales from local to national, and should be set in a range of contexts in different parts of the world. Contexts should include the United Kingdom and the European Union.

■ **7. Rivers**

In studying rivers and their effects on the landscape, pupils should be taught:

a that rivers have sources, channels, tributaries and mouths, that they receive water from a wide area, and that most eventually flow into a lake or the sea;

b how rivers erode, transport and deposit materials, producing particular landscape features, *eg valleys, waterfalls*.

■ 8. Weather

In studying how weather varies between places and over time, pupils should be taught:

a how site conditions can influence the weather, *eg temperatures in the shade and in the sun, wind speed in sheltered and exposed sites*;

b about seasonal weather patterns;

c about weather conditions in different parts of the world, *eg temperatures, rainfall and sunshine conditions in the localities studied, extremes of weather in other parts of the world.*

■ 9. Settlement

In studying how settlements differ and change, pupils should be taught:

a that settlements, *eg villages, towns, cities*, vary in size and that their characteristics and locations reflect the types of economic activities in the settlement, *eg market towns, ports, seaside resorts*;

b how land in settlements is used in different ways, *eg for housing, transport, industry*;

c about a particular issue arising from the way land is used, *eg different groups of residents in a settlement have conflicting views on the construction of a by-pass across farmland.*

■ 10. Environmental change

In investigating how environments change, pupils should be taught:

a how people affect the environment, *eg by quarrying, building reservoirs, building motorways*;

b how and why people seek to manage and sustain their environment, *eg by combatting river pollution, by organic farming, conserving areas of beautiful landscape or of scientific value.*

N

| 0 | 50 | 100km |

N

NORTH
SEA

REPUBLIC
OF IRELAND
Dublin

UNITED
KINGDOM

London

Berlin

GERMANY

R. Rhine

Paris

FRANCE

A L P S

ITALY

Madrid

SPAIN

Rome

M E D I T E R R A N E A N   S E A

0   500km

MAP C World: points of reference

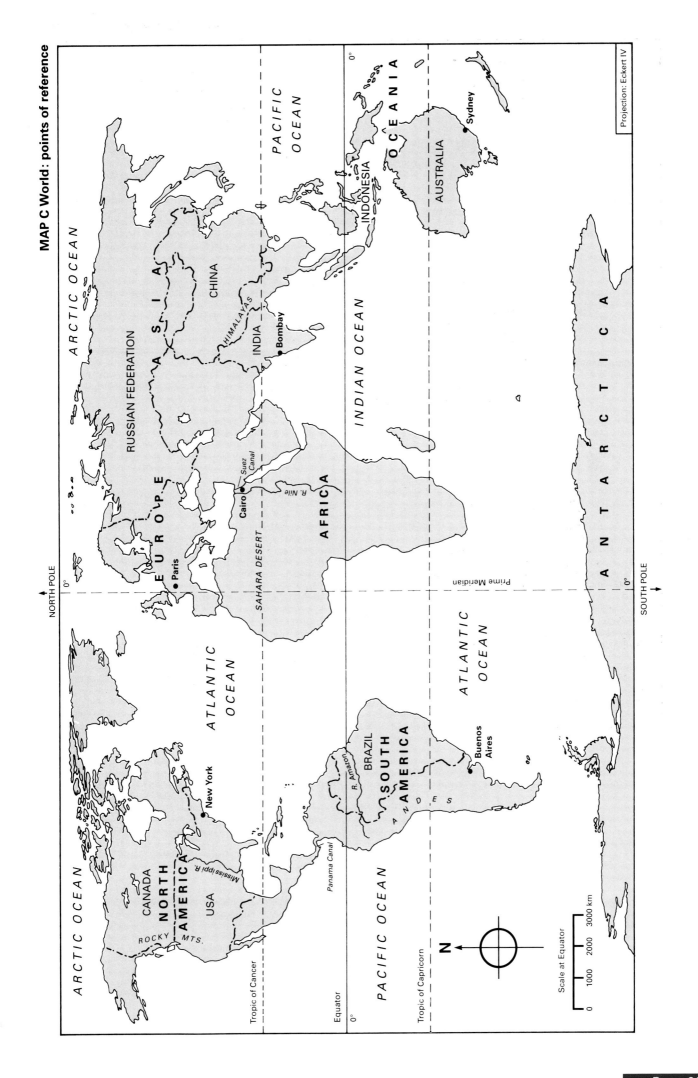

Projection: Eckert IV

ARCTIC OCEAN

EUROPE

ASIA

RUSSIAN FEDERATION

CHINA

HIMALAYAS

INDIA

• Bombay

• Paris

Cairo •

Suez
Canal

R. Nile

SAHARA DESERT

AFRICA

INDIAN OCEAN

INDONESIA

OCEANIA

AUSTRALIA

• Sydney

NORTH POLE

0°

0°
Prime Meridian

SOUTH POLE

0°

ANTARCTICA

ATLANTIC
OCEAN

NORTH
AMERICA

CANADA

USA

Mississippi R.

ROCKY MTS.

• New York

Panama Canal

Tropic of Cancer

Equator

0°

PACIFIC OCEAN

Tropic of Capricorn

SOUTH
AMERICA

BRAZIL

R. Amazon

ANDES

Buenos
Aires •

ATLANTIC
OCEAN

PACIFIC
OCEAN

N

Scale at Equator

0   1000   2000   3000 km

LEVEL DESCRIPTIONS

The following level descriptions describe the types and range of performance that pupils working at a particular level should characteristically demonstrate. In deciding on a pupil's level of attainment at the end of a key stage, teachers should judge which description best fits the pupil's performance. Each description should be considered in conjunction with the descriptions for adjacent levels.

By the end of Key Stage 1, the performance of the great majority of pupils should be within the range of Levels 1 to 3, by the end of Key Stage 2 it should be within the range 2 to 5 and by the end of Key Stage 3 within the range 3 to 7.

■ Level 1

Pupils recognise and make observations about physical and human features of places. They express their views on features of the environment of a locality that they find attractive or unattractive. They use resources provided and their own observations to respond to questions about places.

■ Level 2

Pupils describe physical and human features of places, recognising those features that give places their character. They show an awareness of places beyond their own locality. They express views on attractive and unattractive features of the environment of a locality. Pupils select information from resources provided. They use this information and their own observations to ask and respond to questions about places. They begin to use appropriate vocabulary.

■ Level 3

Pupils describe and make comparisons between the physical and human features of different localities. They offer explanations for the locations of some of those features. They show an awareness that different places may have both similar and different characteristics. They offer reasons for some of their observations and judgements about places. They use skills and sources of evidence to respond to a range of geographical questions.

■ Level 4

Pupils show their knowledge, understanding and skills in relation to studies of a range of places and themes, at more than one scale. They begin to describe geographical patterns and to appreciate the importance of location in understanding places. They recognise and describe physical and human processes. They begin to show understanding of how these processes can change the features of places, and that these changes affect the lives and activities of people living there. They describe how people can both improve and damage the environment. Pupils draw on their knowledge and understanding to suggest suitable geographical questions for study. They use a range of geographical skills, drawn from the Key Stage 2 or Key Stage 3 programme of study, and evidence to investigate places and themes. They communicate their findings using appropriate vocabulary.

■ Level 5

Pupils show their knowledge, understanding and skills in relation to studies of a range of places and themes, at more than one scale. They describe and begin to offer explanations for geographical patterns and for a range of physical and human processes. They describe how these processes can lead to similarities and differences between places. Pupils describe ways in which places are linked through movements of goods and people. They offer explanations for ways in which human activities affect the environment and recognise that people attempt to manage and improve environments. Pupils identify relevant geographical questions. Drawing on their knowledge and understanding, they select and use appropriate skills, from the Key Stage 2 or Key Stage 3 programme of study, and evidence to help them investigate places and themes. They reach plausible conclusions and present their findings both graphically and in writing.

■ Level 6

Pupils show their knowledge, understanding and skills in relation to a wide range of studies of places and themes, at various scales. They explain a range of physical and human processes. They describe ways in which processes operating at different scales create geographical patterns and lead to changes in places. They describe and offer explanations for different approaches to managing environments and appreciate that different approaches have different effects on people and places. Drawing on their knowledge and understanding, pupils identify relevant geographical questions and suggest appropriate sequences of investigation. They select and make effective use of a wide range of skills, from the Key Stage 3 programme of study, and evidence in carrying out investigations. They present conclusions that are consistent with the evidence.

PROGRAMMES OF STUDY

COMMON REQUIREMENTS

■ Access

The programme of study for each key stage should be taught to the great majority of pupils in the key stage, in ways appropriate to their abilities.

For the small number of pupils who may need the provision, material may be selected from earlier or later key stages where this is necessary to enable individual pupils to progress and demonstrate achievement. Such material should be presented in contexts suitable to the pupil's age.

Appropriate provision should be made for pupils who need to use:

- means of communication other than speech, including computers, technological aids, signing, symbols or lip-reading;

- non-sighted methods of reading, such as Braille, or non-visual or non-aural ways of acquiring information;

- technological aids in practical and written work;

- aids or adapted equipment to allow access to practical activities within and beyond school.

  Appropriate provision should be made for those pupils who need emphasis placed on a tactile approach to art, craft and design.

  Judgements made in relation to the end of key stage descriptions should allow for the provision above, where appropriate.

■ Use of language

Pupils should be taught to express themselves clearly in both speech and writing and to develop their reading skills. They should be taught to use grammatically correct sentences and to spell and punctuate accurately in order to communicate effectively in written English.

■ Information technology

Pupils should be given opportunities, where appropriate, to develop and apply their information technology (IT) capability in their study of art, craft and design.

■ Referencing

The numbers and letters throughout the programmes of study are for referencing purposes only and do not necessarily indicate a particular teaching sequence or hierarchy of knowledge, understanding and skills.

■ Examples

Examples printed in italics are non-statutory.

> Art should be interpreted as 'art, craft and design' throughout.
>
> Pupils' understanding and enjoyment of art, craft and design should be developed through activities that bring together requirements from both **Investigating and Making** and **Knowledge and Understanding**, wherever possible.

1. Pupils should be given opportunities to experience different approaches to art, craft and design, including those that involve working individually, in groups and as a whole class.

2. In order to develop visual perception, pupils should be taught the creative, imaginative and practical skills needed to:

   a express ideas and feelings;

   b record observations;

   c design and make images and artefacts.

3. In order to develop visual literacy, pupils should be taught about the different ways in which ideas, feelings and meanings are communicated in visual form.

4. Throughout their work, pupils should be taught about visual and, where appropriate, tactile elements, including:

   a pattern and texture in natural and made forms;

   b colour matching and how colour is mixed from primary colours;

   c how images are made using line and tone;

   d the use of shape, form and space in images and artefacts.

5. Pupils should be introduced to the work of artists, craftspeople and designers, *eg drawing, painting, printmaking, photography, sculpture, ceramics, textiles, graphic design, architecture*, in order to develop their appreciation of the richness of our diverse cultural heritage. The selection should include work in a variety of genres and styles from:

   a the locality;

   b the past and present;

   c a variety of cultures, Western and non-Western.

6. Pupils should be taught to use materials, tools and techniques for practical work safely and in accordance with health and safety requirements.

Investigating and Making

7. Pupils should be given opportunities to:

a record responses, including observations of the natural and made environment;

b gather resources and materials, using them to stimulate and develop ideas;

c explore and use two- and three-dimensional media, working on a variety of scales;

d review and modify their work as it progresses;

8. Pupils should be taught to:

a record what has been experienced, observed and imagined;

b recognise images and artefacts as sources of ideas for their work;

c select and sort images and artefacts, and use this source material as a basis for their work;

d experiment with tools and techniques for drawing, painting, printmaking, collage and sculpture, exploring a range of materials, including textiles;

e experiment with visual elements, *eg pattern, texture, colour, line, tone, shape, form, space*, to make images and artefacts, using the range of media in 8d;

f review what they have done and describe what they might change or develop in future work.

Knowledge and Understanding

9. Pupils should be taught to:

e develop understanding of the work of artists, craftspeople and designers, applying knowledge to their own work;

a identify in the school and the locality the work of artists, craftspeople and designers;

b recognise visual elements, *eg pattern, texture, colour, line, tone, shape, form, space*, in images and artefacts;

c recognise differences and similarities in art, craft and design from different times and places;

f respond to and evaluate art, craft and design, including their own and others' work.

d respond to the ideas, methods or approaches used in different styles and traditions;

e describe works of art, craft and design in simple terms, and explain what they think and feel about these.

Art should be interpreted as 'art, craft and design' throughout.

Pupils' understanding and enjoyment of art, craft and design should be developed through activities that bring together requirements from both **Investigating and Making** and **Knowledge and Understanding**, wherever possible.

1. Pupils should be given opportunities to experience different approaches to art, craft and design, including those that involve working individually, in groups and as a whole class.

2. In order to develop visual perception, pupils should be taught the creative, imaginative and practical skills needed to:

    a express ideas and feelings;

    b record observations;

    c design and make images and artefacts.

3. In order to develop visual literacy, pupils should be taught about the different ways in which ideas, feelings and meanings are communicated in visual form.

4. Throughout their work, pupils should be taught about visual and, where appropriate, tactile elements, including:

    a the use of pattern and texture in designing and making;

    b how colour is applied and experienced in images and designs;

    c different qualities of line and tone in images;

    d how shape, form and space are presented in images and artefacts.

5. Pupils should be introduced to the work of artists, craftspeople and designers, *eg drawing, painting, printmaking, photography, sculpture, ceramics, textiles, graphic design, architecture*, in order to develop their appreciation of the richness of our diverse cultural heritage. The selection should include work in a variety of genres and styles from:

    a the locality;

    b the past and present;

    c a variety of cultures, Western and non-Western.

6. Pupils should be taught to use materials, tools and techniques for practical work safely and in accordance with health and safety requirements.

Investigating and Making

7. Pupils should be given opportunities to:

a record responses, including observations of the natural and made environment;

b gather resources and materials, using them to stimulate and develop ideas;

c explore and use two- and three-dimensional media, working on a variety of scales;

d review and modify their work as it progresses;

8. Pupils should be taught to:

a develop skills for recording from direct experience and imagination, and select and record from first-hand observation;

b record observations and ideas, and collect visual evidence and information, using a sketchbook;

c experiment with ideas for their work suggested by visual and other source material;

d experiment with and develop control of tools and techniques for drawing, painting, printmaking, collage and sculpture, exploring a range of materials, including textiles;

e experiment with and use visual elements, *eg pattern, texture, colour, line, tone, shape, form, space,* to make images and artefacts for different purposes, using the range of media in 8d;

f reflect on and adapt their work in the light of what they intended and consider what they might develop in future work.

Knowledge and Understanding

9. Pupils should be taught to:

e develop understanding of the work of artists, craftspeople and designers, applying knowledge to their own work;

a identify in the school and the locality the materials and methods used by artists, craftspeople and designers;

b identify how visual elements, *eg pattern, texture, colour, line, tone, shape, form, space,* are used in images and artefacts for different purposes;

c recognise ways in which works of art, craft and design reflect the time and place in which they are made;

d compare the ideas, methods or approaches used in different styles and traditions;

f respond to and evaluate art, craft and design, including their own and others' work.

e express ideas and opinions, developing an art, craft and design vocabulary, and the ability to use knowledge to support views.

END OF KEY STAGE DESCRIPTIONS

The following descriptions describe the types and range of performance that the majority of pupils should characteristically demonstrate by the end of the key stage, having been taught the relevant programme of study. The descriptions are designed to help teachers judge the extent to which their pupils' attainment relates to this expectation. The expectations match the level of demand in other subjects and are broadly equivalent to Level 2 at Key Stage 1 and Level 4 at Key Stage 2.

■ Attainment Target 1: Investigating and Making

Pupils record their ideas and feelings confidently and show a developing ability to represent what they see and touch. They choose resources and materials for their visual and tactile qualities to stimulate and develop ideas for their work. They work practically and imaginatively with materials, tools and techniques, and present their work in two and three dimensions.

■ Attainment Target 2: Knowledge and Understanding

Pupils describe and compare images and artefacts in simple terms. They recognise differences in methods and approaches used and make links with their own art, craft and design work.

Key Stage 2

■ Attainment Target 1: Investigating and Making

Pupils record what they have experienced and imagined, expressing ideas and feelings confidently. They represent chosen features of the world around them with increasing accuracy and attention to detail. They select relevant resources and materials and experiment with ideas that are suggested by these. They experiment with, and show increasing control over, a range of materials, tools and techniques. They choose materials and methods and visual elements appropriate to their intentions, making images and artefacts for different purposes. They reflect on and adapt their work, identifying ways in which it can be developed and improved.

■ Attainment Target 2: Knowledge and Understanding

Pupils compare images and artefacts, using an art, craft and design vocabulary, and identify similarities and differences in methods and approaches. They begin to recognise how works of art, craft and design are affected by their purpose, including, where appropriate, the intentions of the artist, craftsperson or designer, and the time and place in which they are made. They evaluate their own and others' work in the light of what was intended.

PROGRAMMES OF STUDY

COMMON REQUIREMENTS

■ Access

The programme of study for each key stage should be taught to the great majority of pupils in the key stage, in ways appropriate to their abilities.

For the small number of pupils who may need the provision, material may be selected from earlier or later key stages where this is necessary to enable individual pupils to progress and demonstrate achievement. Such material should be presented in contexts suitable to the pupil's age.

Appropriate provision should be made for pupils who need to use:

- means of communication other than speech, including computers, technological aids, signing, symbols or lip-reading;
- non-sighted methods of reading, such as Braille, or non-visual or non-aural ways of acquiring information;
- technological aids in practical and written work;
- aids or adapted equipment to allow access to practical activities within and beyond school.

Appropriate provision should be made for pupils with hearing impairment, who need to use equipment and resources that visually record and display sounds.

Judgements made in relation to the end of key stage descriptions should allow for the provision above, where appropriate.

■ Use of language

Pupils should be taught to express themselves clearly in both speech and writing and to develop their reading skills. They should be taught to use grammatically correct sentences and to spell and punctuate accurately in order to communicate effectively in written English.

■ Information technology

Pupils should be given opportunities, where appropriate, to develop and apply their information technology (IT) capability in their study of music.

■ Referencing

The numbers and letters throughout the programmes of study are for referencing purposes only and do not necessarily indicate a particular teaching sequence or hierarchy of knowledge, understanding and skills.

■ Examples

Examples printed in italics are non-statutory.

Pupils' understanding and enjoyment of music should be developed through activities that bring together requirements from both **Performing and Composing** and **Listening and Appraising** wherever possible.

Music

Key

Stage 1

■ **1. Pupils should be given opportunities to:**

a use sounds and respond to music individually, in pairs, in groups and as a class;

b make appropriate use of IT to record sounds.

■ **2.** When performing, composing, listening and appraising, pupils should be taught to listen with concentration, exploring, internalising, *eg hearing in their heads*, and recognising the musical elements of:

a pitch — high/low;

b duration — long/short; pulse or beat; rhythm;

c dynamics — loud/quiet/silence;

d tempo — fast/slow;

e timbre — quality of sound, *eg tinkling, rattling, smooth, ringing*;

f texture — several sounds played or sung at the same time/one sound on its own;

and the use of the above within

g structure — different sections, *eg beginning, middle, end*; repetition, *eg repeated patterns, melody, rhythm*.

■ **3.** The repertoire chosen for performing and listening should extend pupils' musical experience and knowledge, and develop their appreciation of the richness of our diverse cultural heritage. It should include music in a variety of styles:

a from different times and cultures;

b by well known composers and performers, past and present.

Performing and Composing

4. Pupils should be given opportunities to:

a control sounds made by the voice and a range of tuned and untuned instruments;

b perform with others, and develop awareness of audience, venue and occasion;

c compose in response to a variety of stimuli, and explore a range of resources, *eg voices, instruments, sounds from the environment*;

d communicate musical ideas to others;

5. Pupils should be taught to:

a sing songs from memory, developing control of breathing, dynamics, rhythm and pitch;

b play simple pieces and accompaniments, and perform short musical patterns by ear and from symbols;

c sing unison songs and play pieces, developing awareness of other performers;

d rehearse and share their music making;

e improvise musical patterns, *eg invent and change patterns whilst playing and singing*;

f explore, create, select and organise sounds in simple structures;

g use sounds to create musical effects, *eg to suggest a machine or a walk through a forest*;

h record their compositions using symbols, where appropriate.

Listening and Appraising

e listen to, and develop understanding of, music from different times and places, applying knowledge to their own work;

6. Pupils should be taught to:

a recognise how sounds can be made in different ways, *eg by blowing, plucking, shaking, vocalising*;

b recognise how sounds are used in music to achieve particular effects, *eg to soothe, to excite*;

c recognise that music comes from different times and places;

f respond to, and evaluate, live performances and recorded music, including their own and others' compositions and performances.

d respond to musical elements, and the changing character and mood of a piece of music by means of dance or other suitable forms of expression;

e describe in simple terms the sounds they have made, listened to, performed, composed or heard, including everyday sounds.

Pupils' understanding and enjoyment of music should be developed through activities that bring together requirements from both **Performing and Composing** and **Listening and Appraising** wherever possible.

Music

Key

Stage 2

■ **1. Pupils should be given opportunities to:**

   a use sounds and respond to music individually, in pairs, in groups and as a class;

   b make appropriate use of IT to explore and record sounds.

■ **2.** When performing, composing, listening and appraising, pupils should be taught to listen with attention to detail, and identify musical ideas, investigating, internalising, *eg hearing in their heads*, and distinguishing the musical elements of:

   a pitch   —   gradations of pitch, *eg sliding up/down, moving by step/leap; names for pitch such as C, G, doh, soh*;

   b duration   —   groups of beats, *eg in 2s, 3s, 4s, 5s*; rhythm;

   c dynamics —   different levels of volume; accent;

   d tempo   —   different speeds, *eg lively/calm, slower/faster than*;

   e timbre   —   different qualities, *eg harsh, mellow, hollow, bright*;

   f texture   —   different ways sounds are put together, *eg rhythm on rhythm; melody and accompaniment; parts that weave; blocks of sound, chords*;

   and the use of the above within

   g structure —   different ways sounds are organised in simple forms, *eg question and answer; round; phrase; repetition; ostinato (a musical pattern that is repeated many times); melody*.

■ **3.** The repertoire chosen for performing and listening should extend pupils' musical experience and knowledge, and develop their appreciation of the richness of our diverse cultural heritage. It should include music in a variety of styles:

   a from different times and cultures, *eg from the European 'classical' tradition; folk and popular music; the countries and regions of the British Isles; cultures across the world*;

   b by well known composers and performers, past and present.

Key Stage 1

■ Attainment Target 1: Performing and Composing

Pupils sing a variety of songs and play simple pieces and accompaniments with confidence and awareness of pulse. They explore, select and order sounds, making compositions that have a simple structure and make expressive use of some of the musical elements including dynamics and timbre.

■ Attainment Target 2: Listening and Appraising

Pupils respond to short pieces of music, recognising repetition and changes within the musical elements. They listen attentively and describe and compare sounds and pieces of music using simple terms.

Key Stage 2

■ Attainment Target 1: Performing and Composing

Pupils perform accurately and confidently, making expressive use of the musical elements and showing awareness of phrase. They sing songs and rounds that have two parts, and maintain independent instrumental lines with awareness of the other performers. They select and combine appropriate resources, use musical structures, make expressive use of musical elements and achieve a planned effect. They use symbols when performing and communicating musical ideas.

■ Attainment Target 2: Listening and Appraising

Pupils respond to music, identifying changes in character and mood, and recognise how musical elements and resources are used to communicate moods and ideas. They evaluate their own work, identifying ways in which it can be improved. They begin to recognise how music is affected by time and place, including, where appropriate, the intentions of the composer(s) and performer(s). They listen with attention to detail and describe and compare music from different traditions, using a musical vocabulary.

END OF KEY STAGE DESCRIPTIONS

The following descriptions describe the types and range of performance that the majority of pupils should characteristically demonstrate by the end of the key stage, having been taught the relevant programme of study. The descriptions are designed to help teachers judge the extent to which their pupils' attainment relates to this expectation. The expectations match the level of demand in other subjects and are broadly equivalent to Level 2 at Key Stage 1 and Level 4 at Key Stage 2.

Performing and Composing

4. Pupils should be given opportunities to:

a control sounds made by the voice and a range of tuned and untuned instruments;

b perform with others, and develop awareness of audience, venue and occasion;

c compose in response to a variety of stimuli, and explore a range of resources, *eg voices, instruments, sounds from the environment*;

d communicate musical ideas to others;

e listen to, and develop understanding of, music from different times and places, applying knowledge to their own work;

f respond to, and evaluate, live performances and recorded music, including their own and others' compositions and performances.

5. Pupils should be taught to:

a sing songs, developing control of diction and musical elements, particularly phrasing, *eg giving shape to a song by breathing at the end of a phrase*;

b play pieces and accompaniments and perform musical patterns by ear and from notations, *eg symbols which define musical elements*, with increasing dexterity and control;

c sing songs, including songs and rounds in two parts, and play pieces which have several parts, developing the ability to listen to the other performers;

d rehearse and present their own projects/performances;

e improvise rhythmic and melodic ideas, *eg add a percussion part to a song*;

f explore, create, select, combine and organise sounds in musical structures, *eg using repeated sections or verse and chorus*;

g use sounds and structures to achieve an intended effect, *eg to create a particular atmosphere*;

h refine and record their compositions using notation(s), where appropriate.

Listening and Appraising

6. Pupils should be taught to:

a identify the sounds made by a variety of instruments individually and in combination, *eg classroom instruments and families of instruments*;

b identify how musical elements and resources, *eg voices, instruments, performers*, can be used to communicate a mood or effect;

c recognise ways in which music reflects the time and place in which it is created;

d compare music from contrasting musical traditions, and respond to differences in character and mood, *eg through dance or other suitable forms of expression*;

e express ideas and opinions about music, developing a musical vocabulary and the ability to use musical knowledge to support views.

PROGRAMMES OF STUDY

COMMON REQUIREMENTS

■ Access

The programme of study for each key stage should be taught to the great majority of pupils in the key stage, in ways appropriate to their abilities.

For the small number of pupils who may need the provision, material may be selected from earlier or later key stages where this is necessary to enable individual pupils to progress and demonstrate achievement. Such material should be presented in contexts suitable to the pupil's age.

Appropriate provision should be made for pupils who need to use:

- means of communication other than speech, including computers, technological aids, signing, symbols or lip-reading;
- non-sighted methods of reading, such as Braille, or non-visual or non-aural ways of acquiring information;
- technological aids in practical and written work;
- aids or adapted equipment to allow access to practical activities within and beyond school.

  Appropriate provision should be made for those pupils who need activities to be adapted in order to participate in physical education.

  Judgements made in relation to the end of key stage descriptions should allow for the provision above, where appropriate.

■ Use of language

Pupils should be taught to express themselves clearly in speech.

■ The Curriculum Cymreig

In Wales, pupils should be given opportunities, where appropriate, in their study of physical education to develop and apply their knowledge and understanding of the cultural, economic, environmental, historical and linguistic characteristics of Wales.

■ Referencing

The numbers and letters throughout the programmes of study are for referencing purposes only and do not necessarily indicate a particular teaching sequence or hierarchy of knowledge, understanding and skills.

■ Examples

Examples printed in italics are non-statutory.

GENERAL REQUIREMENTS FOR PHYSICAL EDUCATION: KEY STAGES 1–4

Physical education should involve pupils in the continuous process of planning, performing and evaluating. This applies to all areas of activity. The greatest emphasis should be placed on the actual performance aspect of the subject. The following requirements apply to the teaching of physical education across all key stages.

1. To promote physical activity and healthy lifestyles, pupils should be taught:

    a to be physically active;

    b to adopt the best possible posture and the appropriate use of the body;

    c to engage in activities that develop cardiovascular health, flexibility, muscular strength and endurance;

    d the increasing need for personal hygiene in relation to vigorous physical activity.

2. To develop positive attitudes, pupils should be taught:

    a to observe the conventions of fair play, honest competition and good sporting behaviour as individual participants, team members and spectators;

    b how to cope with success and limitations in performance;

    c to try hard to consolidate their performances;

    d to be mindful of others and the environment.

3. To ensure safe practice, pupils should be taught:

    a to respond readily to instructions;

    b to recognise and follow relevant rules, laws, codes, etiquette and safety procedures for different activities or events, in practice and during competition;

    c about the safety risks of wearing inappropriate clothing, footwear and jewellery, and why particular clothing, footwear and protection are worn for different activities;

    d how to lift, carry, place and use equipment safely;

    e to warm up for and recover from exercise.

In each year of the key stage, pupils should be taught three areas of activity: Games, Gymnastic Activities and Dance, using indoor and outdoor environments where appropriate. In addition, schools may choose to teach Swimming in Key Stage 1 using the programme of study set out in Key Stage 2.

Throughout the key stage, pupils should be taught:

- about the changes that occur to their bodies as they exercise;
- to recognise the short-term effects of exercise on the body.

Physical Education

Key Stage 1

AREAS OF ACTIVITY

Pupils should be taught:

1. Games

a   simple competitive games, including how to play them as individuals and, when ready, in pairs and in small groups;

b   to develop and practise a variety of ways of sending (including throwing, striking, rolling and bouncing), receiving and travelling with a ball and other similar games equipment;

c   elements of games play that include running, chasing, dodging, avoiding, and awareness of space and other players.

2. Gymnastic activities

a   different ways of performing the basic actions of travelling using hands and feet, turning, rolling, jumping, balancing, swinging and climbing, both on the floor and using apparatus;

b   to link a series of actions both on the floor and using apparatus, and how to repeat them.

3. Dance

a   to develop control, co-ordination, balance, poise and elevation in the basic actions of travelling, jumping, turning, gesture and stillness;

b   to perform movements or patterns, including some from existing dance traditions;

c   to explore moods and feelings and to develop their response to music through dances, by using rhythmic responses and contrasts of speed, shape, direction and level.

Pupils should be taught six areas of activity. During each year of the key stage pupils should be taught Games, Gymnastic Activities and Dance. At points during the key stage pupils should be taught Athletic Activities, Outdoor and Adventurous Activities, and Swimming unless they have already completed the programme of study for Swimming during Key Stage 1. If aspects of the Swimming programme have been taught during Key Stage 1, pupils should be taught the Key Stage 2 Swimming programme starting at the appropriate point.

Throughout the key stage, pupils should be taught:

- how to sustain energetic activity over appropriate periods of time in a range of physical activities;
- the short-term effects of exercise on the body.

AREAS OF ACTIVITY

Pupils should be taught:

■ 1. Games

a   to understand and play small-sided games and simplified versions of recognised competitive team and individual games, covering the following types – invasion, *eg mini-soccer, netball*, striking/fielding, *eg rounders, small-sided cricket*, net/wall, *eg short tennis*;

b   common skills and principles, including attack and defence, in invasion, striking/fielding, net/wall and target games;

c   to improve the skills of sending, receiving, striking and travelling with a ball in the above games.

■ 2. Gymnastic activities

a   different means of turning, rolling, swinging, jumping, climbing, balancing and travelling on hands and feet, and how to adapt, practise and refine these actions, both on the floor and using apparatus;

b   to emphasise changes of shape, speed and direction through gymnastic actions;

c   to practise, refine and repeat a longer series of actions, making increasingly complex movement sequences, both on the floor and using apparatus.

■ 3. Dance

a   to compose and control their movements by varying shape, size, direction, level, speed, tension and continuity;

b   a number of dance forms from different times and places, including some traditional dances of the British Isles;

c   to express feelings, moods and ideas, to respond to music, and to create simple characters and narratives in response to a range of stimuli, through dance.

Pupils should be taught:

■ 4. Athletic activities

a to develop and refine basic techniques in running, *eg over short distances, over longer distances, in relays*, throwing, *eg for accuracy/distance*, and jumping, *eg for height/distance*, using a variety of equipment;

b to measure, compare and improve their own performance.

■ 5. Outdoor and adventurous activities

a to perform outdoor and adventurous activities, *eg orienteering exercises*, in one or more different environment(s), *eg playground, school grounds, parks, woodland, seashore*;

b challenges of a physical and problem-solving nature, *eg negotiating obstacle courses*, using suitable equipment, *eg gymnastic or adventure play apparatus*, whilst working individually and with others;

c the skills necessary for the activities undertaken.

■ 6. Swimming

a to swim unaided, competently and safely, for at least 25 metres;

b to develop confidence in water, and how to rest, float and adopt support positions;

c a variety of means of propulsion using either arms or legs or both, and how to develop effective and efficient swimming strokes on the front and the back;

d the principles and skills of water safety and survival.

ATTAINMENT TARGET

END OF KEY STAGE DESCRIPTIONS

The following descriptions describe the types and range of performance that the majority of pupils should characteristically demonstrate by the end of the key stage, having been taught the relevant programme of study. The descriptions are designed to help teachers judge the extent to which their pupils' attainments relate to this expectation. The expectations match the level of demand in other subjects and are broadly equivalent to Level 2 at Key Stage 1 and Level 4 at Key Stage 2.

Key Stage 1

Pupils plan and perform simple skills safely, and show control in linking actions together. They improve their performance through practising their skills, working alone and with a partner. They talk about what they and others have done, and are able to make simple judgements. They recognise and describe the changes that happen to their bodies during exercise.

Key Stage 2

Pupils find solutions, sometimes responding imaginatively, to the various challenges that they encounter in the different areas of activity. They practise, improve and refine performance, and repeat series of movements they have performed previously, with increasing control and accuracy. They work safely alone, in pairs and in groups, and as members of a team. They make simple judgements about their own and others' performance, and use this information effectively to improve the accuracy, quality and variety of their own performance. They sustain energetic activity over appropriate periods of time, and demonstrate that they understand what is happening to their bodies during exercise.

Physical
Education

End of

Key Stage

Descriptions

Page 118